*Law*Basics

# COMMERCIAL LAW

*Other titles in the Series*

Agency
Constitutional Law
Contract Law
Evidence

*Law*Basics

# COMMERCIAL LAW

By

Nicholas J.M. Grier, M.A., LL.B., W.S., F.R.S.A.,

*Solicitor,*
*Lecturer in Law,*
*Napier University*

EDINBURGH
W. GREEN/Sweet & Maxwell
1998

First published 1998

Published in 1998 by W. Green & Son Limited of
21 Alva Street,
Edinburgh, EH2 4PS

Typeset by Trinity Typesetting,
Edinburgh

Printed in Great Britain by Redwood Books,
Trowbridge, Wiltshire

No natural forests were destroyed to make this product; only farmed timber was
used and replanted.

A CIP catalogue record of this book is available from the British Library.

ISBN 0 414 01290 9

# TABLE OF CONTENTS

# TABLE OF STATUTES

# 1. SALE AND SUPPLY OF GOODS

## THE NEED FOR LEGISLATION

Traditionally, the sale of goods was regulated by the old Roman law maxim of *caveat emptor* — let the buyer beware. As this was clearly no longer satisfactory for the consumer, legislation was introduced to modernise the law, resulting in the Sale of Goods Act 1979. Other legislation has been enacted to provide further rights for the consumer, amongst these being the Unfair Contract Terms Act 1977, the Sale and Supply of Goods Act 1994, the Consumer Credit Act 1974, the Consumer Protection Act 1987 and the Unfair Terms in Consumer Contracts Regulations 1994, introduced following the 1993 E.C. Council Directive on Unfair Terms in Consumer Contracts.

## THE SALE OF GOODS ACT 1979 ("SOGA")

In order to understand SOGA it is worth understanding the various definitions used throughout SOGA, and indeed throughout the rest of this chapter.

### Definitions
*Goods* means corporeal moveables, which in Scotland means physical, tangible and transportable assets including things growing on or subsisting within land and which can be detached or extracted from land in order to be sold (SOGA, ss. 61). The term "goods" does not include money, except in the context of antique coins and banknotes. It is not entirely clear whether or not computer programs contained on disks fall within the definition of "goods" (as stated in *St Albans City and District Council v. International Computers Ltd* (1995)), or are a species of material which is neither goods nor any other legally recognised form of asset (*Beta Computers (Europe) Ltd v. Adobe Systems (Europe) Ltd* (1996)).

A significant feature of goods is whether they are existing, ascertained and specific goods selected by the buyer, or *unascertained* goods, which are goods not specially chosen or identified by or for the buyer but which are or have been available to the buyer for purchase. When a buyer personally selects a pound of carrots which he presents to the greengrocer for purchase, he has entered into a contract for specific or ascertained goods: if he sends some money to the greengrocer and asks the greengrocer to send him 7lbs of best porridge oats, the contract is for the sale of unascertained goods up to the moment when the greengrocer selects the porridge oats and sets them aside for the buyer, whereupon the goods become ascertained goods. *Appropriation* is the term used to describe the process of selecting, setting aside or otherwise identifying the goods for the buyer with the buyer's assent.

Goods do not need to exist at the time of sale: if the goods have yet to be obtained or manufactured, they are called *future goods*.

A *sale* is defined in SOGA, s. 2 as a contract by which the seller transfers or agrees to transfer the property in goods to the buyer for a money consideration, called the price. Accordingly a transfer which is reciprocated by a swap is not a sale but a form of barter and is outwith SOGA, since SOGA only deals with payment using money. Sale includes the concept of an immediate transfer or a future transfer ("agreement to transfer").

*Property* means the right of ownership. Ownership is different from possession. A person may own a wheelbarrow, but if he lends that wheelbarrow to a friend the friend has possession but not ownership.

A contract of sale of goods may be *absolute* or *conditional* (SOGA, s. 2(3)). An absolute contract of sale is one where the property is transferred without anything needing to be done first. A conditional sale is one where some act needs to be fulfilled, or some time needs to have elapsed before the sale can take place. Where the transfer of the property is to take place after the completion of some act, or after a period of time, the contract is not a contract of sale, but an *agreement to sell* (SOGA, s. (2)(5)). An agreement to sell turns into a sale once the conditional act has been performed or the requisite time has elapsed (SOGA, s. 2(6)). For example, the conditional act might be putting the goods into a deliverable state. Once the goods are in a deliverable state, the property in the goods transfers to the buyer.

When goods are said to be in a *deliverable state* the seller has placed the goods in such a state that the buyer is bound under the terms of his contract to take delivery of them. Equally if goods are not in a deliverable state, the purchaser is not bound to accept the goods (unless the contract says otherwise).

*Breach of contract* occurs where a term of the contract is broken by one of the parties to the contract. If a term of the contract is broken by the seller, the buyer is entitled to claim damages for his loss (SOGA, s. 15B(1)(a)), or if it is a very serious breach of a term (known as a material breach) the buyer is entitled to reject the goods (*i.e.* to send them back to the seller without payment) and to treat the contract as repudiated (*i.e.* to refuse to recognise the continued existence of the contract) (SOGA, s. 15B(1)(b)).

A *material* breach is, as stated above, a significant or serious breach as opposed to a trivial or minor breach of a term of the contract. It is clearly difficult to give a categorical definition of what is material and what is not. In order to give guidance on this issue, SOGA, s. 15B(2) states that in a consumer contract (to be explained later) any breach by the seller of a term in the contract as to the quality of the goods or their fitness for the purpose for which they were supplied (SOGA, s. 15B(2)(a)) is a material breach. Within SOGA, s. 15B(2) there are further occasions which are deemed to be material breaches. If a seller sells his goods by description, by perhaps advertising that he has a large quantity of a particular commodity which he describes as being of best quality and newly made, or if he displays a sample of his wares, there is an assumption that the actual goods will indeed entirely correspond with the seller's description and that the bulk of the goods will correspond with the sample. If it turns out that the goods are not of best quality nor new stock, or that the sample is unrepresentative of the inferior bulk, the consumer buyer may treat the goods' deficiencies as a material breach of a term of the contract, and is therefore entitled to reject the goods and claim his money back.

A *consumer contract* is defined in the Unfair Contract Terms Act 1977 ("UCTA") as one where: (a) either the seller or the buyer is a consumer (*i.e.* someone not dealing, or holding himself out as dealing, in the course of a business) and the other party is dealing in the course of a business; and (b) the goods which form the subject of the contract are goods that are of a type ordinarily supplied for private use or consumption (UCTA, s. 25(1)). The emphasis in this definition lies in the consumer not running a business in the goods. Accordingly the definition of "consumer" can in these circumstances include a non-trading limited company or a charitable association. If there is a dispute about the nature of the consumer contract, it is for the party who says that the contract is not a consumer contract to prove that this is the case (UCTA, s. 25(1)).

*Risk* is the term used to denote the exposure of the goods to the danger of loss or damage. From the moment a buyer accepts the risk in goods transferred or to be transferred to him, he should insure against the loss or destruction of the goods; and likewise where the risk lies with the seller he will be responsible for maintaining the goods up to the moment of transfer of risk.

*Damages* is a term to describe the amount the court may award to cover the difference in value between the value of the contract if it had taken place properly and what the actual value turned out to be. In the context of a seller's breach of contract, it is the estimated loss to the buyer directly and naturally resulting, in the ordinary course of events, from the breach (SOGA, s. 53A(1)). Damages in general aim to restore or bring the claimant to the position he ought to be in if the contract is performed properly, but damages are not meant to be penal in nature. Damages will normally amount to the cost of repair or upgrading to the expected standard, or the value of the loss occasioned by the delay or other fault. Interest is usually allowable as part of the damages. Where there has been bodily injury or consequential damage to property as a result of the faulty goods, there may be damages for these as well (SOGA, s. 53A), though such damages are: (a) only available to the buyer and not to others who may be affected by the faulty goods; and (b) may only be claimed against the seller who may not always be in a position to meet a sizeable claim and who in any case may not have manufactured the faulty goods. Unless the seller has specifically had his attention drawn to matters which are important to the buyer (such as the need for the supplied goods to be ready by a certain date because some other matter was dependent on the goods being ready), the seller will not normally be liable for any further economic loss arising out of his delay or fault (*Hadley v. Baxendale* (1854)). However, if the seller is well aware that the goods must be ready by a certain date and knows that the buyer will suffer loss of business as a result of the seller's delay, the seller may be liable for what is known as pure economic loss, which is the loss of profit arising out of the buyer's subsequent transactions with the goods supplied by the seller.

## EXPRESS AND IMPLIED TERMS

In contracts of sale there are usually *express* terms, which are ones clearly spelt out, and *implied* terms. An implied term is one that is deemed to be in the contract unless it is specifically disapplied in the actual contract, and even then the attempt to contract out of the implied term may in certain circumstances be declared void by the courts. The implied terms in SOGA, ss. 12, 13, 14 and 15 all impose strict liability, which means that irrespective of any reasonable precautions the seller may have taken, if the seller breaches the implied terms he will be liable, and it does not matter whose fault caused the breach. If the contract is silent on any of the undernoted matters the implied terms will automatically apply. The implied terms are that:

(a) The seller has the right to sell the goods (SOGA, s. 12(1). So if the goods turn out to be stolen, the buyer may sue the seller for breach of this right, notwithstanding any intervening circumstances. This took place in *Rowland v. Divall* (1923), where the buyer of a car was successfully able to have his entire purchase price returned to him from the seller when it was discovered that the car was stolen and had to be returned to its true owner, notwithstanding that in the meantime he had had three months of driving in the car.

(b) Up to the moment when the property is to pass to the buyer, there is no charge or encumbrance over the goods, or if there is it must be disclosed to the buyer (SOGA, s. 12(2)(a)). A "charge or encumbrance" is a term of English law and means a right over the goods in favour of somebody else. If a seller sold his car which was in a garage being repaired, the buyer might find when he went to pick it up that the garage owner would not release the car until the seller's repair bill was paid; in this event the buyer could sue the seller for breach of this term because of the undisclosed lien over the car in favour of the garage owner.

(c) Irrespective of the time that the property is to pass, the buyer may have quiet possession of the goods except to the extent of any disclosed charge or encumbrance (SOGA, s. 12(2)(b)). In *Niblett Ltd v. Confectioners Materials Co.* (1921), the buyers found that the labelling on tins purchased from the seller infringed a recognised trademark. The labels had thus to be removed and the buyers successfully sued the sellers for breach of the requirement of "quiet possession".

(d) Where either from the terms of the contract, or from the circumstances surrounding the contract, it is apparent that the seller or a disclosed further person does not have full title (*i.e.* ownership or the right to sell), provisions (a), (b) and (c) continue to apply but the seller or other disclosed further person will only be liable to the extent of what he has not disclosed (SOGA, s. 12(3),(4), and 5)).

Unless it is made clear by the seller to the buyer that the seller is only transferring such (limited) right as he may have (as, say, when a receiver is selling a company's assets under the powers given to him under a floating charge) (SOGA, s. 12(3)), any attempt to contract out of SOGA, s. 12; is automatically void under the UCTA, s. 20(1).

Further implied terms are that:

(e) Unless the contract of sale specifically says so, a stipulation as to when payment for the goods must be made is not deemed to be "of the essence of the contract" (*i.e.* a material matter which will entitle the seller to claim that the contract has been breached) (SOGA, s. 10(1)).

(f) Goods sold by description will correspond with their description (SOGA, s. 13(1)). The bulk of goods should correspond with any sample (as well as with their description if appropriate) (SOGA, s. 13(2)) and even if a buyer selects his goods, his purchase may if necessary still be a sale by description if the buyer has relied on a description.

(g) Where goods are sold in the course of a business (but not necessarily otherwise), the goods supplied must be of "satisfactory quality" (SOGA, s. 14(2)). This phrase replaces the old and confusing term "merchantable quality". Satisfactory is defined as meeting the standard that a reasonable person would regard as satisfactory, taking account of the description of the goods, the price ( where relevant) and all other relevant circumstances (SOGA, s. 14(2A)). "Quality" means the state and condition of the goods (SOGA, s. 14(2B)), taking into account the fitness for the purpose for which the goods were supplied, the goods' appearance and finish, freedom from minor defects, safety and durability (SOGA, s. 14(2B)(a) to (e)). These definitions considerably advance the cause of the consumer. However, if defects or unsatisfactory matters are especially drawn to the buyer's attention, or where the buyer examines the goods and he ought to have noticed the defects, or in the case of a sample if a reasonable examination of the sample would have made the defects apparent, the protection afforded by SOGA, s. 14(2) as to satisfactory quality is withdrawn (SOGA, s. 14(2C)).

(h) Where the buyer explains to the seller (which word in this context also includes credit broker) the purpose for which the goods are being bought, the goods will be reasonably fit for that purpose (even if that purpose is not the usual use for those goods) *unless* circumstances show that the buyer was not relying on the seller's skill and judgment in satisfying that purpose or where it was unreasonable of him to rely on the seller's skill and judgment (SOGA, s. 14(3)). In *Griffiths v. Peter Conway Ltd* (1939), the buyer bought a coat which irritated her very sensitive skin, but would not have irritated other people's skin. She claimed damages for the ensuing dermatitis. It was held that the coat itself was of satisfactory quality (or as it was then, merchantable quality) (SOGA, s. 14(2)) even if it was not satisfactory for her. If she had wished to claim the protection of s. 14(3) she ought to have explained to the seller that she suffered from sensitive skin, and this she had failed to do; it was unreasonable of her to have relied on the seller's skill and judgment where she had not mentioned her skin's sensitivity to him.

(i) The above terms apply to a seller's agents in the course of the seller's business, and to agents for sellers not in the course of business, unless the fact that the seller is not in the course of business is already known to the buyer, or the fact of the seller's not being in business is brought to the attention of the buyer (SOGA, s. 14(5)).

(j) Where there is a sale by sample, the bulk will correspond with the sample in quality and the goods will be free from any defect making the quality of the goods unsatisfactory, which would not be apparent on a reasonable examination of the sample (SOGA, s. 15).

### The exclusion of implied terms

It is not possible in any contract of sale to which SOGA applies to contract out of SOGA, s. 12 (UCTA, s. 20(1)) except, as stated above, to the extent that someone who does not have full title discloses his title as being less than full and discloses all charges in which case the only person who may destroy the buyer's possession of the goods is the disclosed holder of the charge (SOGA, s. 12(4), (5)). It is also not possible to contract out of the provisions of SOGA, ss. 13 to 15 (referred to in paragraphs (f) to (j) above) in a consumer contract (UCTA, s. 20 (2)), though it is possible to do so in a commercial or non-consumer contract if the relevant contracting-out clause is fair and reasonable as defined in UCTA, s. 24. This states that to define what is fair and reasonable, regard should be had to the circumstances known to, or which ought reasonably to have been known to, the parties at the time the contract was made. Reference may also be made to UCTA, Schedule 2 which lays down various guidelines as to: (a) the abuse of any strength of bargaining power; (b) the effect of any inducements to accept the contracting out clause; (c) normal business practice in the trade concerned or between the parties; (d) the practicality of compliance with any condition without which liability would be excluded; and (e) whether the goods were specially made or adapted to the buyer's particular order.

As regards the contracting out from implied terms (other than those specified in the previous paragraph), it is open to the parties to make such provisions as they choose, either expressly, by course of dealing, or by "such usage as binds both parties to the contract", being actions which indicate that both parties do intend to be bound by any contracting-out of the relevant implied terms and have an interest in being contracted-out (SOGA, s. 55(1)).

### Further exclusion clauses

Under the Unfair Terms in Consumer Contracts Regulations 1994 ("UTCCR"), where consumers are required to enter into contracts where the opportunity for individual negotiation is not available (as in standard term contracts for such things as satellite televisions, portable telephones, etc.), consumers will not be bound where a term is "unfair". Unfairness is judged by the criteria of being contrary to the requirements of good faith, being significantly in favour of the non-consumer party to the contract, and being detrimental to the consumer (UTCCR, reg. 4 (1)). In addition, as with the fairness test in the above paragraph, attention must be paid to the relative bargaining power of the parties and any inducements made in exchange for the exclusion clause.

## CAPACITY TO BUY AND SELL

Not everyone is legally empowered to enter into contracts generally, and this is governed by the normal rules of contract. Some individuals are *incapax* which means that by virtue of mental incapacity or other cause they are incompetent to contract. Where such individuals are sold necessaries (*i.e.* items such as food, drink and clothing) they must pay (and indeed are only obliged to pay) a reasonable price for them (SOGA, s. 3(2)). The law on sales to children is regulated by the Age of Legal Capacity (Scotland) Act 1991 ("ALC"). Children below the age of 16 have no contractual capacity and their guardians (normally their parents) must act on their behalf. However, below the age of 16 it is acceptable for them to enter into contracts appropriate to their age and on terms that are "not unreasonable" (ALC, s. 2(1)). Children aged 16 or over may enter into contracts of sale and purchase in the normal manner, except that between the ages of 16 and 17 if a contract is prejudicial to the child's interest the courts may set it aside at any stage up to the child's 21st birthday if a prudent adult would not have entered into the contract on the terms that the child suffered (ALC, s. 3(1),(2)). If the child has lied about his age in order to enter the contract he will not be protected, and if he is in the course of a business he also loses the protection of the statute (ALC, s. 3(3)).

FORMATION OF CONTRACTS OF SALE

Contracts for sale may be made verbally, in writing, by a combination of these means or may be inferred from the actions of the parties to the sale (SOGA, s. 4). In any event the implied terms, referred to above, are deemed to be part of the contract of sale (except where variation of the implied terms is both agreed by the parties and permissible, which in the case of consumer contracts it may not be). As with all contracts, there must be *consensus in idem* (agreement on the same matters), a buyer and a seller, both with the necessary legal capacity, a price (which in the absence of any other agreement must be reasonable under the circumstances (SOGA, s. 8)) and goods (present or future) to be transferred along with the property in the goods. Where specific goods have perished without the knowledge of the seller before or at the time that the contract is made, there are clearly no goods so the contract is void (SOGA, s. 6) and no contract of any sort exists. Where there is an agreement to sell specific goods and goods subsequently perish through no fault of the buyer or seller before the risk passes to the buyer, the agreement is "frustrated" (*i.e.* cannot be brought to fruition) or avoided, the contract terminated and the seller has no obligation to deliver the goods (SOGA, s. 7) and any money the buyer had given to the seller for the now perished goods would have to be returned to the buyer. This rule does not apply in the case of unascertained goods, since the seller ought to be able to produce more (unperished) goods from his warehouse. As stated above goods generally must be of satisfactory quality and fit for the relevant purpose for which they were acquired.

**When does the buyer get the property in the goods ?**
This depends whether or not the goods are unascertained. If the goods are unascertained, no property in the goods passes to the buyer until the goods are ascertained (SOGA, s. 16). Where the goods are specific or ascertained,

the property in the goods passes when the parties intend the property to pass. This will normally be established by the terms of any written or oral contract, the conduct of the parties and any other circumstances (SOGA, s. 17). However, sometimes buyers and sellers are not as careful as they should be and do not expressly state when they intend the property to pass, and in the absence of any other expressed intention, SOGA, s. 18 has set up five rules which may be used to establish the intention of the parties. These are as follows:

(1) Where there is an unconditional contract for the sale of specific goods in a deliverable state, the property passes to the buyer when the contract is made, irrespective of any delay in the time of payment or delivery.

(2) Where there is a contract for the sale of specific goods and the seller has yet to put the goods into a deliverable state, the property does not pass until the goods are in a deliverable state and the buyer has been informed of the fact.

(3) Where there is a contract for the sale of specific goods in a deliverable state but the goods need to be measured in order to ascertain the price, the property does not pass until the measurement has taken place and the buyer has been informed of the fact.

(4) When goods are supplied on approval or on sale or return the property does not pass until (a) the buyer tells the seller of his approval (or by another action adopts the sale); or (b) if the buyer does not signify his approval or acceptance but retains the goods without notice of rejection beyond any specified period for rejection, or in the absence of a specified time, beyond a reasonable period. The sort of action that presupposes acceptance is using the goods as security for some other transaction or hiring the goods to another person. It should be explained that this rule is unconnected with "inertia selling", the practice of sending unsolicited goods and subsequently intimidating unwilling recipients of the goods into buying the goods. This is forbidden under the Unsolicited Goods and Services Act 1971.

(5) Where there is a contract for the sale of unascertained or future goods by description, and where goods of that description and in a deliverable state are "unconditionally appropriated" to the contract (*i.e.* irrevocably set aside for the contract without there being any outstanding conditions which have first to be fulfilled) by the seller with the buyer's agreement, or by the buyer with the seller's assent, the property in the goods passes to the buyer when the goods are appropriated (rule 5(1)). The assent may be done expressly or by implication (*i.e.* through the actions of the parties) and may take place either before, at or after the appropriation. Unconditional appropriation may also take place where the seller delivers the goods to the buyer or to someone on the buyer's behalf such as a carrier without reserving to himself the right to dispose of the goods (rule 5(2)). Where there is a

contract for the sale of a specified quantity of unascertained goods in a deliverable state which forms part of a bulk agreed upon by the parties, and where for some reason the bulk is reduced from its original quantity but the buyer is the only remaining person due to receive goods from that bulk, the remaining quantity of the goods is to be taken as appropriated to the contract and the property therein passes to the buyer (rule 5(3)). This rule arose out of problems in the delivery of various commodities, especially where the seller had gone into liquidation. It effectively allows the goods to be ascertained by exhaustion, by taking what is remaining after other persons have taken from the bulk what is due to them even though no actual act of ascertainment by the buyer has taken place.

These five rules apply where there is no contrary indication in the contract. But there is nothing to prevent the seller retaining a right of disposal until the fulfilment of some condition (SOGA, s. 19). A common example of this is a retention of title clause in a contract for the supply of goods, retaining the property in the goods with the seller until all sums due by the buyer to the seller are paid — even though the buyer may be in possession of the goods. Under SOGA, s. 25(1) if the buyer disregards the retention of title clause and sells the goods anyway, any sub-buyer buying the goods in good faith and without notice of the retention of title clause is entitled to keep the goods and cannot be compelled to return them (*Archivent Sales and Development Ltd v. Strathclyde Regional Council* (1985), discussed later).

### When does risk pass?

Unless there is some agreement to the contrary, the normal rule is that the risk in the goods remains with the seller until the property is transferred to the buyer, irrespective of the date of delivery to the buyer (SOGA, s. 20(1)). In *Pignatoro v. Gilroy* (1919), the buyer acquired bags of rice but failed to uplift them from the seller's premises. When the bags were stolen from those premises the buyer had to bear the loss. This rule, while clear, is perhaps surprising since normally the person who has possession of the goods has the greatest interest in them, as in a hire purchase agreement. Consequently, as a matter of practice it is prudent always in any contract to clarify when risk passes, who will have the benefit of any insurance over the goods and who is paying the insurance premiums.

As exceptions to the general rule above, if there has been any delay in the delivery of the goods, and the delay is attributable to one of the parties to the contract, the goods are at the risk of the party at fault to the extent of the loss which arose as a result of the fault (SOGA, s. 20(2)), and secondly, sellers and buyers acting as custodiers or carriers cannot rely on the above general rule to avoid the duty to take adequate care of the goods while goods are in their care or in transit (SOGA, s. 20(3)).

### Transfer of title

If someone obtains goods which he does not own, and sells those goods without the authority or consent of the owner, the buyer gets no better title than the person purporting to sell the goods (SOGA, s. 21(1)), also known by the Latin phrase *nemo dat quod non habet* (no one can give what he does not own). So if a thief sells stolen goods, the buyer may be required to hand the goods back to the true owner and sue (if he can) the thief for the value of the goods that he had to relinquish. This rule is disapplied where the owner's own conduct prevents him from objecting to the seller's right to sell the goods (SOGA, s. 21(1)). This is known in Scotland as personal bar (in England, estoppel) and very rarely happens in practice, except perhaps where an owner has permitted his agent to sell the owner's goods and then changes his mind. This rule is also disapplied where goods are being sold following a poinding or other court order, or where agents are acting on the owner's behalf even though the owner had withdrawn his authority (SOGA, s. 21(2)).

Where the seller of goods has a voidable title (*i.e.* a title that could be challenged, as when a buyer obtains goods by fraud as opposed to theft) but that title has not been reduced at the time he sells the goods to a buyer, the seller may transfer title to the goods to a buyer who buys in good faith and without notice of the seller's defect in title (SOGA, s. 23). This arose in *Macleod v. Kerr* (1965), where Kerr sold his car to a rogue named Galloway who paid for the car with a stolen cheque. Galloway promptly sold the car to Macleod and in the meantime Galloway's cheque was dishonoured. Kerr sued Macleod to get his car back, but it was held that Kerr had failed to take sufficient steps quickly enough to reduce Galloway's voidable title. Kerr had informed the police but had not told Galloway of his fraud. His only remedy was to sue Galloway, and Macleod was able to retain the car. The significance of this case is that the unfortunate Kerr ought, in theory, to have communicated more quickly with Galloway (who was no doubt keeping well out of the way) in order to reduce the contract between Galloway and Kerr. The other significant feature is that section 23 only applies in the context of a voidable title. Where the contract is void from the beginning, because, for example, there is error in the identity of the buyer (as in *Cundy v. Lindsey* (1878), or the Scottish case of *Morrisson v. Robertson* (1908)), section 23 does not apply and the original owner will be able to retrieve his goods from the person possessing the goods.

In the context of hire purchase, where a purported seller of a motor vehicle being acquired under a hire purchase agreement (but not under a contract of lease) sells that vehicle, a buyer (other than a car dealer) buying it in good faith without notice of the finance company's interest in the vehicle may obtain good title to the goods (Hire-Purchase Act 1964, s. 27(1),(2)). The exception relating to car dealers arises because of a perception that car dealers are well able to look after their own interests without the extra benefit of consumer protection.

Where a seller has sold goods to a buyer and received payment for the goods, but the goods are in the possession of the seller, if the seller inadvertently or fraudulently transfers or delivers the goods to a new buyer buying in good faith and without knowledge of the fact that the goods belong to the first buyer, the new buyer gets good title to the goods (SOGA, s. 24). The old buyer is then entitled to sue the seller for damages for non-delivery. Where a seller delivers goods to a buyer who then delivers or transfers the goods to a sub-buyer who buys the goods in good faith and without any notice of the rights of the original seller, the sub-buyer obtains good title to the goods (SOGA, s. 25(1)). In *Archivent Sale and Development Ltd v. Strathclyde Regional Council* (1985), the seller delivered goods to a contractor carrying out work at a school. The contractor sold on the goods to the school, despite not having paid the original seller who had attempted to safeguard his position with a retention of title clause. As the goods had been transferred to the school's owners, who had acquired the goods in good faith and without knowledge of the rights of the original seller, the seller was unable to assert his claim to the goods. Accordingly section 25(1) limits the applicability of retention of title clauses. This rule does not, however, apply in the context of conditional sale agreements regulated under the Consumer Credit Act 1974, s. 25 or in the context of acquisitions by car dealers (as referred to above).

### How is the contract of sale to be carried out ?

It is the duty of the seller to deliver the goods and the duty of the buyer to accept the goods and to pay for them, all in accordance with the terms of the contract for the sale of the goods (SOGA, s. 27). Unless the contract says otherwise, delivery and payment are concurrent, and both parties should be ready to perform their parts of the contract simultaneously. There are varied and pragmatic rules to govern such matters as where delivery is to take place (SOGA, s. 29), the delivery of more or less goods than had been requested (SOGA, s. 30) (more of the required quantity entitles the buyer to reject the excess, very much more entitles the buyer to reject it all; if too little is delivered, the buyer must pay at the contracted rate for what he receives and claim damages for non-performance of the rest of the contract, while delivery of much too little entitles the buyer to reject it all), delivery by instalments (SOGA, s. 32) and delivery to carriers, where generally delivery to the carrier is deemed to be delivery to the buyer; but in each of these events the precise details may be varied by agreement between the parties. Where the seller delivers goods to the buyer, the buyer must be allowed a reasonable time to examine the goods to see if they conform to the contract or to see if the bulk of the goods match previously seen samples (SOGA, s. 34). He is not held to have accepted the goods until he has been afforded these opportunities for examination even if he has signed an acceptance receipt (SOGA, s. 35(2)). In a consumer contract, a consumer is not deprived of this right even if apparently made to do so by the terms of his contract (SOGA, s. 35(3)). The buyer is held to have accepted the goods where he tells the seller he has done so (SOGA, s. 35(1)(a)), or where he treats the goods in a manner which is inconsistent with the ownership of the seller, for example, where he uses them as security for some other transaction. If a buyer retains the goods for a reasonable time without telling the seller that he is rejecting them, he is deemed to have accepted the goods (SOGA, s. 35(4)). If the buyer asks the seller to repair the goods, the request does not signify acceptance (SOGA, s. 35 (6)(a)); and even if the goods are delivered to someone else through a subsale the buyer may still be entitled to reject the goods within a reasonable time (SOGA, s. 35(6)(b)). It remains to be seen what is meant by a "reasonable time". Where the goods are units within a bigger and ultimately indivisible set of goods, as, for example, one print within a narrative series of prints all within a limited edition, the acceptance of the one item is deemed to be an acceptance of all the items (SOGA, s. 35(7)).

### The buyer's right of rejection

The buyer may if necessary reject the goods, except where he has accepted the goods in the circumstances outlined in the previous paragraph, or where the breach by the seller of a term of the contract is not sufficiently material to entitle the buyer to reject the goods (SOGA, s. 15B). Accordingly, if the courts decide in a case that the time for rejection of delivered goods is past, but the goods are still not to the buyer's satisfaction in terms of quality, the buyer's remaining remedy, assuming the claim is justified, is damages arising out of the loss directly and naturally resulting from the breach of the contract in terms of quality (SOGA, s. 53A). It is sometimes possible to both claim damages and to reject the goods (SOGA, s. 15B). Unless the terms of the contract say otherwise, it is possible to have partial rejection, where the buyer could reject all of an entire consignment of goods but instead chooses to keep the satisfactory goods and reject the unsatisfactory goods (SOGA, s. 35A). This rule applies both in respect of a single delivery or delivery by instalments. Formerly it was only possible to reject all the goods or none of them. If a buyer legitimately rejects goods, he is not bound to return them to the seller unless the terms of the contract of sale say otherwise. He must, however, intimate his rejection to the seller (SOGA, s. 36). If the buyer after a reasonable time delays or refuses to accept the goods when he should properly do so, the buyer is liable to the seller for the cost of storage and care of the goods (SOGA, s. 37).

### Other rights for the buyer

Where the seller neglects or refuses to deliver the goods to the buyer, the buyer may claim damages for non-delivery (SOGA, s. 51). Equally, in the case of a contract of sale of specific or ascertained goods, the buyer may raise an action of specific implement to enforce delivery of the goods (SOGA, s. 52). This means that the court pronounces an order compelling the seller to perform his part of the contract.

### The seller's rights

Where a seller has not been paid (known as the "unpaid seller") he is entitled to retain the goods until payment while he possesses the goods, even if the property in the goods has transferred to the buyer, and in the event of the insolvency of the buyer, he may also stop any goods that are in transit to the buyer (SOGA, s. 39(1)(a) and (b)). Where some of the goods have been delivered by the unpaid seller to the buyer, but the remainder has not, the seller may withhold delivery of the remainder pending payment. The unpaid seller also has a right of resale (SOGA, s. 39(2)), subject to intimation to the buyer giving him a reasonable time within which to make payment. These rights may be abrogated by the terms of the contract, as where an arbitration clause takes effect. Where the seller is no longer in possession of the goods or they are still in transit to the buyer as above, he may raise an action for the price (SOGA, s. 49(1)), or claim damages for non-acceptance where the buyer ought properly to have accepted and paid for the goods (SOGA, s. 50).

## DELICTUAL LIABILITY

### Problems with SOGA, s. 14 and the duty of care

If a seller sells goods whose defects cause damage to the buyer, the seller incurs strict liability under SOGA, s. 14. However, the buyer may sue only the seller for the goods' defects, as opposed to suing the manufacturer (who may be better placed to meet any claim), and only the buyer can sue the seller. So if a buyer bought goods as a present for his uncle, his uncle could not sue the seller for any injury to him caused by the goods. What the buyer can sue for is the estimated loss directly and naturally arising in the ordinary course of events from the breach (SOGA, s. 53A) and any consequential losses where those cause damage to the buyer personally or to his property.

Accordingly where injured non-buyers wish to raise an action against a seller, or where an injured buyer or non-buyer wishes to raise an action against the manufacturer, he must make a claim for negligence arising out of a breach of the manufacturer's duty of care, as in *Donoghue v. Stevenson* (1932). Where there are defective components in manufactured goods, the claimant ( the "pursuer" in a Scots claim) may raise an action under the Consumer Protection Act 1987 ("CPA"), which provides for strict liability for defective products. This Act is derived from the E.C. Product Liability Directive 85/374 and serves to provide a remedy for anyone who suffers damage from a defective product produced by a producer (commonly a manufacturer). It is not possible to contract out of the strict liability provisions (CPA, s. 7) though it is possible for the victim to be contributorily negligent whereupon any damages payable by the producer will be abated to the extent of the victim's own negligence (CPA, s. 4, referring to the Law Reform (Contributory Negligence) Act 1945 and the Fatal Accidents Act 1976, s. 5).

### The liability of producers

Suppliers of products, if they are not manufacturers themselves, may be held liable where they unreasonably delay or refuse to identify who the true producer is (CPA, s. 2(3)), although this rule does not apply where goods are supplied other than in the course of a business, in order to protect the parties in private transactions (CPA, s. 4(1)(c)). Companies that produce their "own brand" products, such as supermarkets, are treated as if they were producers themselves unless they make it clear who the actual manufacturer is (CPA, s. 2(2)(b)). Importers bringing in goods from outside the European Union are treated as constructive producers (CPA, s. 2(2)(c)). The word "product" does not include buildings though it does include items fitted into buildings, so that, say, a defective heating system that gased a consumer could give rise to compensation (CPA, s. 46). There is no requirement to prove that a manufacturer is negligent in order to assert a claim: it is enough to prove that the product was defective, *i.e.* that its safety is not such as persons generally are entitled to expect (CPA, s. 3(1)), and safety in this context applies to property as well as to personal injury or death (CPA, s. 3(1)).

### Protection for the manufacturer and the "state of the art" defence

When this Act was under consideration it was recognised that too strict an application of the principle for the requirement of safety could lead to a stifling of inventive talent, and so there are safeguards in CPA, s. 4 to protect the producer:

(a)  where the goods are manufactured in compliance with E.C. safety rules;

(b)  where the products were used without the producer's authority (as when the products have been stolen);

(c)  where the products have not been supplied in a commercial transaction;

(d)  where the fault is attributable to some other producer's misuse of the products; or

(e)  where the fault lies in the overall design which is not of the producer's making (CPA s. 4(1),(2)).

The most significant safeguard is the "state of the art" defence in CPA, s. 4(1)(e) that the defect was such that given the state of scientific and technical knowledge at the time, a similar producer of similar products would also have been unaware of the defect. This is an objective test and the producer's own knowledge of other businesses or of scientific and technical matters is not enough: the producer, irrespective of his own resources, is expected to be aware of the most recent developments in the area of the product and cannot rely on his own ignorance.

### Prohibition on small claims and on claims for pure economic loss

The damages that are available are for personal injury or damage to property including land, though to discourage small claims, only claims where the damages would amount to more than £275 will be entertained by the court (CPA, s. 5(4)). CPA, s. 5 prohibits claims for pure economic loss, so that if, say, a component in a lawnmower breaks down, the pursuer can neither claim for the faulty component in the lawnmower nor for the cost of the repair to the lawnmower as a whole (CPA, s. 5(2)). However, if the component in the lawnmower caused damage to the owner or to somebody else or to other property, that damage would be an allowable claim. Where damage is caused by a faulty component added at a later date to the lawnmower, but which was not originally part of the lawnmower, it is possible to claim for the damage to the lawnmower as a result of the faulty component (since it is now treated as "property"), though it is not possible to claim for the value of the actual component itself. This is because the claim for the actual component could be made under SOGA, s. 14. CPA serves to provide a remedy of damages arising out of physical injury to people or damage to property but is not concerned with obtaining damages which could be used to pay for the cost of the faulty component itself.

## CRIMINAL LIABILITY

In addition to the civil law protection for the consumer outlined above, there is a large body of criminal law designed to protect the consumer. The main Acts dealing with this matter are the Trade Descriptions Act 1968 and Parts II and III of the CPA, though there are many others which have an important part to play such as the Weights and Measures Act 1965 and Financial Services Act 1986. Errant producers or sellers, as the case may be, may suffer criminal penalties for breach of the legislation.

### The Trades Descriptions Act 1968 ("TDA")

This act prohibits false trade descriptions (TDA, s. 1) which are false to a material degree (TDA, s. 3(1)) or, where not false, are misleading (TDA, s. 3(2)). A false description need not be in writing: an oral representation is sufficient (TDA, s. 4(2)) and applies equally to advertisements as to the actual goods (TDA, s. 6). TDA does not just apply to goods; it applies also to services (TDA, s. 14). There are criminal sanctions for any offences contravening the TDA which can apply both to individuals and to the company employing those individuals (TDA, s. 20), although it is recognised that there are difficulties in making a company liable for the aberrant actions of its employees particularly when the employees have been well warned of the need to obey the law (see *Tesco Supermarkets Ltd v. Nattrass* (1972), but also *Re Supply of Ready-Mixed Concrete (No.2)* (1995)). However, at the time of writing the whole area of corporate liability for criminal actions is being re-examined and is likely ultimately to be the subject of further legislation. There are defences to TDA if it can be proved that the accused was mistaken as the result of someone else's fault (TDA, s. 24(1)(a)) and that it was reasonable for him to rely on that other person, providing that other person has been identified to the court (TDA, s. 24(2)), or that the mistake was a matter otherwise beyond the accused's control. There is also a defence of "due diligence" open to the accused where he has been prosecuted for breach of the legislation (TDA, s. 24(1)(b)): due diligence requires that the fault lies not with the accused but with some other person who failed to pass on the relevant information or to carry out some required act, and that the accused "took all reasonable precautions and exercised all due diligence" (*i.e.* did all that could reasonably be expected of him) to prevent the fault occurring. It is therefore wise for businesses to set up proper training methods and procedures to ensure that misleading advertisements do not occur. Advertising agents and newspapers printing other people's advertisements are not liable for misleading advertisements providing that they had no reason to suspect their publication would lead to an offence under TDA (TDA, s. 25). The local Weights and Measures Inspectorate and Trading Standards Authorities ("TSA") have powers to enter premises and make test purchases to ensure that TDA is being properly complied with. However, if the officers of the Inspectorate or the TSA seize goods or other items which are subsequently found not to have contravened the requirements of TDA, the Inspectorate or TSA must compensate the owner for any loss that he suffers.

### Consumer safety under CPA, Part II

Producers' breaches of consumer safety may result in prosecution (CPA, s. 10). Under the CPA it is a defence to prosecution for breach of consumer safety requirements to state that the accused reasonably believed that the goods were not being used or consumed in the United Kingdom, or that at the time of offering the goods for sale in the course of his business as a retail trader he neither knew, nor had reasonable grounds for believing, that the goods failed to comply with the safety requirement, or that he did not offer the goods as new and that those buying the goods intended to buy the goods in their imperfect state (CPA, s. 10(4)). The Secretary of State has power to make regulations to provide for consumer safety and this is normally done in consultation with retail organisations, manufacturers and the Health and Safety Commission (CPA, s. 11(5)). Adherence to these regulations is naturally advantageous to the accused facing prosecution (CPA, s. 10(3)). Under such regulations there may be, initially, prohibitory notices and notices to warn in order to dissuade the producer or seller from selling the unsafe goods (CPA, s. 13), but if that is insufficient, suspension notices may be served on anyone selling goods which may be in breach of the safety regulations (CPA, s. 14). Where the enforcement authority has made a mistake and there is no contravention the enforcement authority is required to compensate the supplier of the goods (CPA, s. 14(7)). It is open to the relevant authorities to seize and forfeit the accused's goods where they fail to comply with the required standards (CPA, s. 17).

### Misleading price indications under CPA, Part III

Under Part III of the CPA, it is a criminal offence for a person to give misleading information to consumers about the prices at which goods, services, accommodation or other facilities may be available (CPA, s. 20(1)). As "misleading" is inherently an uncertain word, section 21 indicates that a price indication is misleading if it fails to state what a consumer might reasonably expect it to cover, if it suggests that the price is less than it actually is, if it fails to include additional charges or fails to detail facts or circumstances which have a bearing on the price, thus ensuring that it is difficult for the consumer to compare prices. Part III extends to the provision of services, including banking, insurance, foreign currency transactions, electricity, parking and caravan residence (CPA, s. 22). CPA does not, however, apply to contracts of employment, investment services or the sale of new homes (CPA, s. 23). There are defences to Part III, for instance that the accused has complied with non-statutory codes of practices in the relevant industry (such codes having been drawn up in conjunction with the Secretary of State and/or the Director of Fair Trading (CPA, s. 25(2)); that the information is contained in newspaper articles, as opposed to advertisements within newspapers, and is not actionable under the CPA (CPA, s. 24(2)); that publishers of advertisements in newspapers are not liable if they did not know and had no grounds for suspecting that the advertisements were misleading (CPA, s. 24(3)); that the indication as to prices for goods, services, accommodation or facilities did not relate to the availability from the accused of any of those goods and services, etc., as the accused had merely been recommending a price at which the providers of those goods and services, etc. could offer them, that price being reasonable under the circumstances — even if some providers chose not to follow that price so that it appeared to be a misleading price (CPA, s. 24(4)). The accused may also use the due diligence defence in a similar manner to the one referred to above (CPA, s. 39).

As with the TDA, there are provisions for enforcement by authorised officers of the relevant bodies (CPA, s. 27), enabling the officers to make test purchases (CPA, s. 28), search and seize goods and papers (CPA, s. 29) but also to pay compensation where they have failed to obtain a conviction (CPA, s. 34).

**Further reading**
Atiyah, *The Sale of Goods* (9th ed., Pitmans, 1995).
Cusine and Forte, *Scottish Cases in Commercial Law* (2nd ed., Butterworths, 1998).
Gloag and Henderson, *The Laws of Scotland* (10th ed., 1995), Chaps 16 and 17.
Goode, *Commercial Law* (Penguin, 1995), Chap. 14.
Forte (ed.), *Scots Commercial Law* (Butterworths, 1997), Chap. 2.

---

# 2. HIRE OF GOODS

A hire of goods differs from a sale of goods in that during a hire the owner (known as the lessor) retains ownership of the goods and the hirer merely has the use or possession of the goods. At the end of the period of hire possession reverts to the owner. The law relating to hire is mostly covered by the common law and by the Supply of Goods and Services Act 1982 ("SGSA"), the Consumer Credit Act 1974 ("CCA"), the Unfair Contract Terms Act 1977 ("UCTA") and the Unfair Terms in Consumer Contracts Regulations 1994 ("UTCCR").

**Regulated hire agreements**
While the common law regulates contracts of hire generally, a hire agreement involving a consumer (which terms denotes ordinary consumers, sole traders and partnerships but not limited companies (CCA, s. 189(1))), enduring for more than three months, and requiring the consumer/hirer to make payments amounting to less than £15,000 in value is known as a *regulated hire agreement* (CCA, s. 15). This means that the hirer is entitled to the protection of CCA. Consequently the terms of the hire must be properly and clearly set out on appropriately designed forms (CPA, s. 60) which in turn must be properly drawn up and executed in accordance with the regulations of CCA (CCA, s. 61). All regulated hire agreements must be in writing, with copies made available to the hirer (CCA, s. 63), clearly explaining both parties'

rights. Failure to follow the correct procedure and wordings on all documentation may invalidate the hire or delay the enforcement of the lessor's rights of repossession by requiring the lessor to apply to the court (CCA, s. 65). This is to protect the hirer from the sudden and possibly arbitrary repossession of the hired goods and from the requirement to make unexpected termination payments or pay other penalties of which the hirer may have been unaware. There is judicial control of any such attempts at repossession by the use of time orders, giving the hirer time to pay, or even reducing or discharging the sum the hirer is due to pay, all on the principle of fairness to the consumer (CCA, ss. 126–136). Prior to the hire, the hirer is entitled to cancel the agreement during a cooling off period of five days if there have been face to face negotiations prior to the signing of the hire agreement and if the hire agreement has been signed somewhere other than at the lessor's (or his agent's) premises (CCA, s. 68); following cancellation the goods must be returned to the lessor and any hire payments returned to the hirer (CCA, ss. 67–72). There are detailed rules to deal with default by the hirer, requiring notices to be sent to the hirer explaining his default and giving him the opportunity to remedy it (CCA, ss. 87–89) and other rules to cover early repayment (CCA, ss. 94–97) and the termination of the agreement (CCA, ss. 98–104).

Hire agreements which are not regulated hire agreements are covered by SGSA and by the terms of the hire agreement itself, on the grounds that those who can afford to deal in sums greater than £15,000 ought to be able to look after their financial affairs without the state having to help them. Similarly limited companies entering into hire agreements already receive some protection by virtue of their members' limited liability and should not be entitled to any more protection.

### The effect of the Supply of Goods and Services Act 1982

Broadly speaking, SGSA implies into contracts of hire, including regulated hire agreements, many of the same terms that are applied to contracts of sale under SOGA (as detailed in the previous chapter), so that there are implied terms that the hirer has title to lease the goods (SGSA, s. 11H(1)(a)) and that the hirer may enjoy quiet possession of the goods (SGSA, s. 11H(2)). As with SOGA, there are rules to ensure that goods hired on the basis of a description conform to that description (SGSA, s. 11I), that goods hired on the basis sample conform to the bulk (SGSA, s. 11K), and that the goods are of satisfactory quality and fit for their purpose (SGSA, s. 11J).

### The liability of the lessor

It is expected that the hired goods will be serviceable for the duration of the hire, but if repairs are necessary these should be at the lessor's expense, except where the hire agreement says otherwise or where the repairs are necessary because of the hirer's fault. Where the hired goods cause damage to people or property, the lessor is strictly liable under the Consumer Protection Act 1987 in the same manner as a supplier under a contract of sale (see previous chapter at pp. 13–14). He also can suffer the same civil and/or criminal penalties as a supplier should the hired goods derogate from the required standard of safety that can be expected. The lessor cannot contract out of the provisions of UCTA relating to the lessor's liability for personal injury or death arising out of the hired goods (UCTA, s. 16(1)(a)), and any other exclusion clauses will only be acceptable where they are "fair and reasonable" (UCTA, s. 16(1)(b)). Any consumer hire agreement on standard terms which has not been individually negotiated with the hirer may be set aside by the courts (in the same manner as contracts of sale) if the contract is significantly one-sided in favour of the non-consumer party to the contract (*i.e.* the lessor) and there is an element of lack of good faith (UCTTR, reg. 4.1).

### The liability of the hirer
The hirer must pay his hire charges as contracted or, in the absence of a specified rate, at a reasonable rate. In a regulated hire agreement the rates in any event would have to be properly detailed. If the goods are faulty the hirer is normally entitled to deduct a reasonable sum to reflect his inability to use the hired goods satisfactorily. The hirer is under a duty of care to look after the goods properly in the manner that a prudent and sensible person would look after his own property. He would not be responsible for fair wear and tear, but he would be responsible if he wore the goods out through overwork or overuse.

### Further reading
Forte (ed.), *Scots Commercial Law* (Butterworths, 1997), Chap. 2.
Gloag and Henderson, *The Law of Scotland* (10th ed., W.Green, 1995), Chap. 25.
Goode, *Commercial Law* (2nd ed., Penguin, 1995).

---

# 3. CONSUMER CREDIT

### The purpose of the legislation
The Consumer Credit Act 1974 ("CCA") was introduced in order to: (a) provide a new, rational and coherent set of rules regulating the provision of credit; (b) set up a licensing system so that only authorised credit dealers could provide credit; and (c) set out a framework for the proper and fair provision of credit.

The aspects of CCA that deal with hire (as opposed to hire purchase) are dealt with in Chapter 2.

### Licensing requirements
Under CCA, s. 21 only licensed traders, lenders or credit brokers may carry on the business of consumer credit and consumer hire. Under section 147 only licencees may carry out the business of credit brokerage, debt-adjustment, debt-counselling, debt-collecting or the operation of credit reference agencies (known collectively as ancillary credit business). However, an

occasional or "one-off" loan, made by someone not in the course of a business, does not normally require the credit-provider or arranger to be licensed (CCA, s. 189(2)) and certain bodies such as local authorities are exempt from the licence requirement (CCA, s. 21(2)). There are two types of licence, these being a "standard" licence (the more usual) and a group licence (CCA, s. 22(1)). All businesses carrying on licensable credit business, other than those operating through group licences, such as solicitors under the aegis of the Law Society of Scotland, must obtain a standard licence, and each company within a group, as with a bank and its subsidiaries, must obtain a separate standard licence. Licences will only be issued if the Director General of Fair Trading, who supervises the operation of CCA, is satisfied that the licensee is fit to hold a licence. His criteria take into account not only the licensee's business name (lest there be any confusion with any other business of a similar name and nature), but also its compliance and its employees' compliance with the requirements of CCA (CCA, s. 25). There is a public register of licensees, and penalties for carrying on a licensable credit business without a suitable licence (CCA, ss. 39 and 147).

## THE PROTECTION AFFORDED TO THE CONSUMER

### Who is a "consumer"?
In the context of the CCA, a consumer is an individual wishing to enter a credit arrangement of less than £15,000 (CCA, s. 8(2)). Individuals in this context means private persons, partnerships of private persons, unincorporated clubs, charities and societies (CCA, s. 189(1)). Incorporated bodies such as limited companies do not count as individuals except in the context of a joint hire to an individual and a limited company under CCA, s. 185(5).

### The meaning of "credit"?
Credit is a cash loan and any other form of financial accommodation, cash here meaning money in any form (CCA, s. 9(1)). The wording is deliberately wide so that most forms of credit will be caught by the legislation — in the interests of the consumer.

## REGULATED AGREEMENTS

Regulated agreements are any agreements that are regulated by CCA, of which the most common are described below. Under CCA, s. 16 and the Consumer Credit (Exempt Agreements) Order 1989 (S.I. 1989 No. 869)("CC(EA)O"), some credit agreements are exempt from all the regulations, as explained later. It is possible to have some credit arrangements that feature several different types of arrangement, in which case they are known as multiple agreements.

### Consumer credit arrangement
A personal credit arrangement is any agreement between a debtor and a creditor for credit of any amount. This is to be contrasted with a (regulated)

consumer credit arrangement, which is one where the consumer is an individual as defined above and the sum of credit is £15,000 or less (CCA, s. 8(2)), unless it is exempt under CCA, s. 16.

### Hire-purchase

Hire-purchase is treated as a form of credit as, in effect, it spreads the cost of acquiring goods over a period of time by means of regular hire payments followed by an option to purchase (CCA, s. 189(1)). During the period of hire and under the terms of the hire-purchase agreement the consumer is still liable for any damage and for any repairs necessary. If the consumer fails to maintain his monthly payments, the finance company is entitled to repossess the goods and sell them to defray its loss. Where the goods are repossessed, the CCA lays down careful rules to ensure that the consumer is treated fairly in respects of the payments he has already made. Hire-purchase agreements are regulated by the CCA under ss. 9(3),15(1)(a) and 189(1). They are treated as consumer credit agreements for fixed sum credit.

### Running account credit (CCA, s. 10(1)(a))

This is a facility whereby the borrower may borrow up to £15,000. He may make repayments into the account and then borrow again from the account providing that at no stage is the total amount borrowed greater than £15,000.

### Fixed sum credit (CCA, s. 10(1)(b))

This is a less flexible arrangement than a running account credit. With fixed sum credit a sum of money is borrowed in one amount or in instalments. Both of these are extensively used by banks when offering loans to customers. They may be contrasted with overdrafts which are specifically exempt from CCA by virtue of CCA, s. 74.

### Restricted use agreement (CCA, s. 11)

In this situation the credit may only be used for one purpose, as opposed to an *unrestricted use agreement* which may be used for any purpose. Restricted use agreements are common in the situation of hire-purchase agreements where the credit is provided for the one use only, such as the purchase of a car. A restricted use agreement enables the creditor to monitor the debtor's use of the credit more closely, in return for which the creditor may be able to offer a lower interest rate.

### Debtor-creditor-supplier agreement (CCA, s. 12)

This is an agreement between a debtor (usually a customer), a creditor (usually a finance company) and a supplier (often a retailer). A common example of this is a credit card such as Visa or American Express. If a customer buys a computer from a supplier using his credit card, he pays for the computer with the credit facility offered by the credit card company. The credit card company pays the supplier, and the customer will find the cost of the computer on his next statement from the credit card company. He has to pay the amount due on his statement plus any interest if due. The advantage to the supplier is that it knows it will get paid, since a cheque from the customer might not clear; the advantage to the customer is that he can buy the computer quickly and if the supplier defaults, the customer has a joint and several claim against both the supplier and the credit card company, albeit that the credit card company may then be indemnified by the supplier (CCA, s. 75). This is known as connected lender liability. This rule does not apply where the claim relates to an item whose cash price from the supplier is less than £100 or is greater than £30,000. The particular advantage of the CCA, s. 75 is that where the supplier goes into liquidation, the consumer can still claim against the credit card company should he need to do so.

### Credit token agreements (CCA, s. 14)

This is a regulated agreement which applies to such forms of credit as storecards. The credit token does not need to be limited to the one outlet (as with a storecard that only provides credit for the one shop) though that is its common use.

Where a debtor allows someone else to use his credit token, he is liable for any loss to the creditor arising from that use (CCA, s. 84(2)), but when the token is used by an unauthorised person, the debtor is liable up to the sum of £50 to the creditor (CCA, s. 84(1)). If the debtor finds his token has been stolen or otherwise lost and immediately informs the credit-token provider of his loss, liability does not arise (Consumer Credit (Credit Token Agreements) Regulations 1983 (S.I. 1983 No.1055)).

### Credit agreements exempt under CCA (CCA, s. 16)

Certain credit agreements are specifically exempt from the consumer credit legislation. These are:

(a) normal trade credit agreements (excepting hire purchase agreements, land purchase agreements and agreements secured by a pledge) for a fixed sum repayable in no more than four payments within a period of a year (CC(EA)O, art. 3(1)(a)(i)) and for a running account credit agreement (subject to the same exceptions as above) repayable in one lump sum within a designated period(CC(EA)O, art. 3(1)(a)(ii)) — as in a Gold Card or Diners Club card;

(b) land transactions repayable in no more than four repayments (CC(EA)O, art. 3(1)(b));

(c) mortgage lending for the acquisition of land or the securing of a loan upon land (CCA, s. 16(1),(2));

(d) low cost credit, where the cost of the loan is not greater than base rate plus 1 per cent or 13 per cent, which ever is the higher (CC(EA)O, art. 4));

(e) loans for certain insurance policies, usually to pay the premiums on property insurance or mortgage protection policies (CC(EA)O, art. 3));

(f) credit agreements for the financing of exports from or imports into the United Kingdom (CC(EA)O, art. 5));

(g) consumer credit arrangements where the creditor is a housing authority and where the agreement is secured by a standard security on a house (CCA, s. 16(6A)).

The hiring of gas, electricity or water meters is exempt from the legislation (CC(EA)O, art. 6). All other agreements, covered by the CCA and not exempt, are "regulated agreements".

### General rules for regulated agreements

CCA operates to ensure that any advertising carried out by consumer credit businesses is accurate and intelligible, complete with "health warnings" alerting the borrower or hirer to the pealties arising from non-fulfilment of his requirements (CCA, ss. 43–47). The annual percentage charge for credit ("APR") must be clearly visible and include hidden charges. Quotations are similarly closely regulated (CCA, ss. 52–54). Canvassing or soliciting of customers must be fairly done, and may only take place off trade premises under very restricted circumstances (CCA, ss. 48–51). All agreements regulated by CCA have to follow certain specified forms and procedures(CCA, ss. 60–66), one of which is a "cooling-off" period during which time the debtor may change his mind (CCA, s. 68). The debtor is permitted to cancel an agreement within five days of either receiving a copy of the executed agreement (where it was signed off trade premises (CCA, s. 67(a)) or the date when he received notice of the debtor's rights of cancellation intimated to him under CCA, s. 64.

Notwithstanding the above, CCA, s. 74 excludes four types of agreement from the above rules, these being:

(a) non-commercial agreements (*i.e.* one-off non-business loans);
(b) current account overdrafts;
(c) loans in connection with debts due after a death (such as a loan by a bank to pay inheritance tax due by the deceased's estate); and
(d) small agreements for restricted use credit for the provision of credit of less than £50.

With all regulated agreements (other than those exempted by CCA, s. 74), the creditor may not enforce his rights unless he has notified the debtor of his intention to do so by means of a default notice (CCA, s. 87). In the process of enforcing his rights, or should the debtor choose to object to the enforcement, the matter may come before the courts, which may grant a time order for payment (CCA, s. 129) or in the case of hire purchase, a return order or a transfer order (CCA, s. 133). This will normally be a method of allowing the debtor time to pay off his debts by instalments or to remedy any breach (CCA, s. 129). Any lapse by the creditor in the provision of all the necessary forms and documentation for the agreement may make the creditor's application for enforcement invalid, or delay it until the documentation is correct. Anybody granting security or a guarantee as part of any credit transaction will also need to be given the appropriate documentation to ensure that he is aware of the implication of his grant of security (CCA, ss. 105–113).

Under CCA, ss. 98–104 termination of regulated agreements may only be done in accordance with the strict provisions of the Act.

### Pawnbroking

Strict rules apply to pawnbrokers and their documentation with regard to the pawning of goods. The pawnbroker must give each customer a copy of the pawn agreement, a notice of his cancellation rights and a receipt for the pawned goods (CCA, s. 115). The pawn will be redeemable within a period of six months or such longer period as may be agreed (CCA, s. 116), or the goods will pass to the pawnbroker who may sell the goods after intimation to the customer (CCA, s. 121). If after the sale of the goods there is a surplus after repayment of the loan and interest and expenses, the surplus is repayable to the customer (CCA, s. 121(3)). If the sale proceeds are less than the sum due, the balance remains outstanding from the customer to the pawnbroker (CCA, s. 121(4)).

### Extortionate credit transactions

An extortionate credit transaction is a credit transaction which the court decides is extortionate. The court at its discretion, may rewrite the transaction so that a fairer contract subsists. Grounds for deeming a credit transaction extortionate would be unreasonable rates of interest, the borrower's current financial pressures and any other relevant facts about the borrower. If a borrower alleges that the transaction is extortionate, it is for the creditor to prove that it is not (CCA, s. 171(7)).

### Further reading

*Encyclopaedia of Consumer Credit Law* (Sweet & Maxwell).

Ervine, *Consumer Law in Scotland* (W. Green, 1995), pp. 172–224.

Gloag and Henderson, *The Law of Scotland* (10th ed., W. Green, 1995), Chap. 18.

Harding, *Consumer Credit and Consumer Law and Practice* (Sweet & Maxwell, 1995).

*Stair Memorial Encyclopaedia* (Law Society of Scotland/Butterworths, 1987), Vol. 5, paras 801–965.

---

# 4. CAUTION AND GUARANTEES

Caution (pronounced "kay-shun") is the Scots legal term for a guarantee. The term is now falling into disuse except in the context of "lodging caution" which is where the court orders that a party to a court action lodges funds, either in the form of cash or an insurance policy (sometimes known as a "bond of caution") to cover his opponent's costs. As the requirement to lodge caution can give rise to injustice for impoverished litigants, the courts do not lightly use this power.

The more common term for caution nowadays is a guarantee. With a guarantee there must be a debtor who is due money or required to fulfil some other obligation ("the principal debt") for a creditor, who in turn seeks reassurance by way of guarantee from the guarantor that if the debtor defaults, the guarantor will make good any loss to the creditor. The guarantee is ancillary to the principal debt, so that if the debt is extinguished, so too is the guarantee.

Caution is a *ius in personam* and therefore gives the creditor no better rights in the cautioner's assets than any other creditor in the event of the cautioner's insolvency.

## The major uses of guarantees

Guarantees are commonly used: (a) by banks as a form of security from directors personally or a holding company where a new and/or subsidiary company wants to borrow money; (b) by banks on the occasion of the opening of a new bank account for, or a loan to a  possibly unreliable customer; (c) in the form of performance bonds, to ensure the completion of a project in the event of the insolvency of the contractor.

## The form of the guarantee

It may be unwise not to have a guarantee in writing but it is not illegal: it merely leads to problems of proof. However, where a guarantee is gratuitous and is not given in the course of business, it must be in writing (Requirements of Writing (Scotland) Act 1995, s. 1(2)(ii)). Otherwise it may be in writing, or may be evidenced by actings or parole evidence.

There is no standard wording for guarantees, though most bank guarantees will normally state the extent of the guarantor's liability, his requirement to pay any interest and expenses and the duration of the guarantee. Commonly there will be a clause giving warrant for preservation and execution, thus enabling the bank to effect summary (*i.e.* immediate) diligence against the guarantor. Prudent cautioners will insist on only being liable for a fixed sum, or a fixed proportion of the total sum and no more (known as "benefit of division") as opposed to being jointly and severally liable. They will also wish to ensure that the guarantee relates only to a specific transaction as opposed to all of the debtor's transactions generally. Prescription applies to guarantees, and after five years the liability under the guarantee prescribes (Prescription and Limitation (Scotland) Act 1973, s. 6).

## Guarantees for a spouse's debts

Following the case of *Smith v. Bank of Scotland* (1997), and in accordance with current banking codes of practice, if a bank wishes a spouse of a debtor to guarantee the debtor's debts, that spouse must be advised to take independent advice before he or she signs the guarantee. This brings the law in Scotland into line with English practice.

## The cautioner's rights against the debtor

Under the common law, the cautioner is allowed a right of relief against the debtor — for what it is worth. However, it is possible that a debtor may be temporarily unable to satisfy a debt against a creditor so that a guarantee has to be honoured: at a later date the debtor may, say, inherit some money and thus be in a position to relieve the cautioner (*Smithy's Place Ltd v. Blackadder & McMonagle* (1991)). If a cautioner has had fully to honour the guarantee, the creditor must on request assign the benefit of any security or other rights (such as diligence) he may have against the debtor in favour of the cautioner so that the cautioner can the better enforce his right of relief against the debtor (*Thow's Trustees v. Young* (1910)).

## The *contra proferentum* rule

If there is ambiguity in the wording of a guarantee, and one party (usually in practice the creditor) is seeking to rely on the ambiguity of the wording to favour his own interests, the wording is construed in a manner that is contrary to the interest of the person drawing up the contract of guarantee.

## Misrepresentation
Where a debtor induces a cautioner by misrepresentation to sign a guarantee, the guarantee is still valid and the cautioner has a right of action against the debtor, though this may be of little benefit to him (*Young v. Clydesdale Bank* (1889)). A creditor's failure to reveal information about the debtor to the cautioner does not invalidate a guarantee, since it is up to the cautioner to satisfy himself that it is safe to offer a guarantee for the debtor's debts to the creditor (*Royal Bank of Scotland v. Greenshields* (1914)); but if the cautioner actually asks the creditor for information about the debtor (either in writing or orally) the creditor must not misrepresent the position and if the cautioner relies on that misrepresentation, whether it is made fraudulently or innocently, he may resile from the guarantee (*Royal Bank of Scotland v. Ranken* (1844)). In practice it is likely that any creditor given such a request would say that the cautioner must make his own enquiries.

### Termination of the guarantee
Once the principal debt is repaid, the guarantee is discharged. But where the debt is discharged on the debtor's bankruptcy, the guarantee still continues in existence (Bankruptcy (Scotland) Act 1985, s. 60) and indeed will almost certainly be called upon. The benefit of a guarantee may be assigned, unless there is some term in the guarantee forbidding this and providing that the assignation is intimated to the cautioner. During the course of the guarantee the creditor is not permitted to make the cautioner's position worse than the position he had accepted when he entered into the guarantee (see *Huewind Ltd v. Clydesdale Bank plc* (1995), where the cautioner was not released from its guarantee because it was unable to prove that the debtor's increased liability was the bank's fault).

The death of the debtor prevents any further liability under the guarantee, but the cautioner remains liable for whatever he may have contracted for up to that point (*Woodfield Finance Trust (Glasgow) Ltd v. Morgan* (1958)). The death of the cautioner transfers the cautioner's liability to his estate unless the guarantee says otherwise. If there are several cautioners, and one of them is discharged without the others being discharged or without their consent, then all of the cautioners are discharged, unless the guarantee says otherwise (Mercantile Law Amendment (Scotland) Act 1856, s. 9).

### Further reading
Clark and Eden, "Cautionary Obligations" in *Stair Memorial Encyclpedia* (Law Society of Scotland/Butterworths, 1994), Vol. 3.
Forte (ed.), *Scots Commercial Law* (Butterworths, 1997), Chap. 6.
Gloag and Henderson, *The Law of Scotland* (10th ed., W. Green, 1995), Chap. 20.
Wilson, *The Scottish Law of Debt* (2nd ed., W. Green, 1991), Chap. 10.

# 5. NEGOTIABLE INSTRUMENTS

Negotiable instruments are a method, using signed documents, of transferring funds from one person to another, other than by using cash or by modern methods of electronic transfer. The law relating to bills of exchange underpins the law relating to cheques. The word "negotiable" means that a bill may be transferred from one person to another as if it were cash, so that the paper instruction of one person to pay another becomes almost as good as handing cash over in payment for goods.

## The negotiability of bills of exchange

If Alan buys goods costing £10,000 from Ben on February 1, but cannot pay Ben immediately though he expects to be able to do so by March 1, Ben could draw up a bill of exchange that would state that Alan was to pay Ben £10,000 on March 1. Alan would accept the bill, that is, acknowledge that he will have to pay the bill on the due date, and return it to Ben. Ben then has an entitlement to £10,000. If he needs the cash now, he might be able to find someone to whom he could sell the bill, and who in turn could receive the money from Alan. Theoretically Ben could assign his general right of payment to anyone who would be willing to buy that right from him. But if he wished to sell that general right he would have to assign it formally to the buyer and intimate the assignation to Alan — which is cumbersome. The virtue of a bill of exchange is that there is no need for intimation, for (subject to a few exceptions) a bill is treated as a free standing obligation in its own right irrespective of the underlying transaction. Indeed if Ben's goods turned out to be faulty and Alan refused to accept them, the bill of exchange would still be valid and Alan would have to pay the bill of exchange. Ben could transfer or "negotiate" the bill to Charles, who might buy the bill of £10,000 less a discount to take account of Ben's need for cash now, the risk of Alan defaulting on payment, and the loss of a month's interest on £10,000. In turn Charles could sell the bill to David. Even if David had defrauded Charles to obtain the bill, David could still sell the bill on to Edward, who, provided he bought the bill in good faith without notice of there being anything wrong with the bill, and provided the bill was on the face of it valid, could still ultimately receive payment from Alan (assuming Alan had accepted the bill to begin with).

## The nature of a bill of exchange

A bill of exchange is essentially an instruction to one person ("A") by a second person ("B") that the first person should pay a specified sum to a third person ("C") at a specified date. The Bills of Exchange Act 1882 ("BOE"), s. 3 states as follows:

> A bill of exchange is an unconditional order in writing, addressed by one person to another, signed by the person giving it, requiring the person to whom it is addressed to pay on demand or at a fixed or determinable future time a sum certain in money to or to the order of a specified person, or to bearer.

The person who instructs the order, B, is known as the "drawer" of the bill. He must sign the bill or it is invalid. Signing the bill works in two ways: it serves as proof of the instruction to the drawee, A, but it also makes the drawer liable at a later date if the bill is dishonoured (*i.e.* not paid when it should be).

The person who receives the order to pay the bill, A, is known as the "drawee". The process of ordering the payment of the bill is known "as drawing a bill".

The recipient of the money on payment, C, is the "payee". When the bill is first drawn, the payee's name will be stated (unless it is made payable to bearer) and the payee will expect to receive payment. If, however, the payee negotiates the bill to someone else, the original payee loses his entitlement to payment and the new holder of the bill becomes the payee.

"Bearer" means a person who is bearing the bill, *i.e.* has it in his possession. Where a bill is made out to bearer, the bill may be transferred by delivery (BOE, s. 31(2)).

A "holder" is similar to a bearer in that he is a person who is "holding" the bill of exchange, or in other words who has it in his possession, but in addition he is normally entitled to payment on it. Holders are discussed in greater detail later. Bills may not be made out to holder.

The amount payable is stated to be "a sum certain in money". This means exactly what it says, so that the figure stated must be calculable (if there is interest due) and payable in money as opposed to any other commodity.

There must be no conditions attached to the bill or it will lose its status as a bill. The date of payment must be fixed or at least determinable. It is common to have bills payable in periods of 30 days, but it is possible to have a bill payable on demand, or on sight or on presentment. But a time bill, which gives a specific date, may only be paid on or after that date.

**Indorsement**
When a bill that is payable to order is transferred, the practice is for the payee to sign his name on the bill. This is known as indorsement and, when followed by delivery to the transferee, is an effective negotiation of the bill. Alternatively the indorsee in turn might wish to transfer the bill to someone specific, in which case he too would indorse his name and add the words "Pay AB" and hand the bill to AB, the new indorsee. This is known as special indorsement (BOE, s. 34(2)) and limits the transferability of the bill to AB alone, though AB could negotiate it further if he wished to do so. It is possible to restrict the transfer by ascribing the indorser's name and adding "Pay AB only", thus making it a restrictive indorsement (BOE, s. 35(2)). The bill then ceases to be negotiable and if it is negotiated by AB to, say, CD, CD takes no better title than AB. If the bill is made payable to bearer, there is no need for signatures; all that is required is delivery (BOE, s. 31(2)). An order bill ought to be indorsed to show who the indorsee is, but if none is specified, the bill then becomes "blank indorsed" and is treated as a bearer bill (BOE, s. 34(1)). If a blank indorsed bill is stolen, the thief may obtain payment and the victim of the theft would not be

able to get payment. The recipient of a blank indorsed bill could however protect himself by signing his name where it could have been inserted by the indorser, thus converting the blank indorsement into a special indorsement (BOE, s. 34(4)).

A person who indorses a bill has to accept the fact that by indorsing the bill he may have to compensate the indorsee (or subsequent indorser) should the bill not be paid (BOE, s. 55(2)(a)). He may not subsequently assert that he is not liable on the bill because the drawer's signature or any previous indorsers' signatures were forged or irregular (BOE, s. 55(2)(b)) or that he did not have good title to the bill anyway (BOE, s. 55(2)(c)).

## Acceptance by the drawee of the bill

For a bill of exchange to be effective on a practical basis, the drawee must know that he has to pay the bill to the payee. He does this by accepting the bill when it is first sent to him by the drawer. He formally writes on the bill the word "accepted" along with his name. This is not necessary for cheques or promissory notes. The drawee's acceptance of the bill results in his redesignation as an "acceptor", and he will normally then forward the bill to the payee. Without acceptance, the bill may be less valuable because his acceptance is a formal acknowledgment of his awareness of his duty to pay. It is possible to give a qualified acceptance, though a wise payee will refuse it as he is entitled to do (BOE, s. 44(1)), since the condition imposed under the qualification might be something beyond his immediate control.

A drawee may refuse to accept the bill. This is known as dishonour by non-acceptance and it makes the drawer who signed the bill liable instead (BOE, s. 42). This is because it is possible that the drawer has no dealings with the drawee and is effectively trying to defraud the drawee, or mislead the payee into believing that the drawee will pay the payee. If the drawer has transferred the unaccepted bill to subsequent transferees, each of them is potentially liable to the ultimate holder of the bill as well (BOE, s. 43(2)), though the holder must first notify the dishonour to the drawer and to the indorsee (BOE, s. 48) and those who are not notified will not be liable (BOE, s. 48).

Assuming the bill is accepted, in due course the bill will have to be re-presented to the acceptor by the payee or the ultimate holder for payment when the time for payment comes. However, if the acceptor then refuses to pay the bill further steps will be required. These will be discussed shortly.

Where the drawee is a fictitious person or someone without contractual capacity, the drawer will be trying to negotiate a bill that has no underlying obligation on a drawee to pay. So if the drawer tries to negotiate the bill, ultimately he will become liable for it to a subsequent holder of a bill as he should not have drawn the bill on a person who could not pay it (BOE, s. 5(2)).

## THE HOLDER IN DUE COURSE

### The holder
As stated above, the first person due to receive payment under a bill is the payee. Where the payee transfers the bill to someone else, either by indorsement and delivery, or by delivery if the payee is a bearer, the person holding the bill is known as the holder. Even if a fraudster swindles someone into receiving a bill, the fraudster is a holder, though he has a voidable title to the bill. A holder is entitled to present the bill to the acceptor for payment (BOE, s. 45(3)). If the bill is stolen, the bill still remains the property of the former owner, though in practice it becomes very difficult to prevent the holder either selling the bill on to another holder or presenting it to the acceptor for payment. A holder is entitled to sue for payment, but under BOE, s. 38, if there is a defect in the title, he may be unable to assert his claim. So if a thief holding a bill tries to obtain payment of a bill, but the victim told the acceptor first that the bill had been stolen, the acceptor would not need to pay the bill and the thief could not sue the drawer or any subsequent indorsee for payment either. A holder's claim is strengthened if he is (a) a holder for value, and (b) also a holder in due course.

### Holder for value
A holder for value is a person who has paid for it, or where a prior holder has paid for it (BOE, s. 27(1), (2)). This provision is necessary because of the English law of consideration.

### Holder in due course
A holder in due course is in the happy position, as indicated earlier, of being well protected and well able to obtain payment under the bill, provided the following conditions are satisfied under BOE, s. 29(1):

    (a)   the bill must be complete and regular on the face of it, so that as far as can be seen it contains all the essential requirements of a properly drawn up bill;

    (b)   the bill is not overdue;

    (c)   the holder is unaware of any previous dishonour of the bill, either by non-acceptance or non-payment;

    (d)   the holder must have acquired the bill in good faith;

    (e)   the holder must have been unaware of any defect in title in the previous holder who negotiated the bill to him.

If all these criteria are satisfied, the holder becomes a holder in due course and may obtain a better title to the bill than the person who negotiated the bill to him, even if somewhere in the course of the bill's progress it has been obtained fraudulently. If the bill is dishonoured by the acceptor, the holder in due course may claim against the drawer who may then claim against the acceptor (BOE, s. 57(1)). Alternatively, the holder in due course may claim against the indorser who transferred it to him, who in turn may also claim against the acceptor or from the drawer or from a prior indorser

(BOE, s. 5(2)). In theory this ought to mean that eventually the chain of liability should go back to the fraudster, against whom a claim could be made.

## Dishonour

Where a bill is dishonoured, either for acceptance or later for payment, the proper procedure is to have the bill "noted" and "protested", which is a formal procedure before a notary public and which is public notice of the failure of the acceptor to do what he should. The advantage of this is that, at least as regards inland bills, the holder in due course may then exercise summary diligence against the drawer and indorsers to obtain payment (BOE, s. 43).

## Presentment for payment

Presentment for payment is normally made to the acceptor who pays the bill. As stated earlier, a drawee is not obliged to accept (BOE, s. 43(2)) or pay a bill (BOE, s. 48(2)) and thereupon the drawer and indorsers become liable instead, though notice of their liability must be given to each of them (BOE, s. 48). As stated in the previous paragraph, where dishonour for payment takes place, noting and protest is normally required, and then summary diligence may be carried out against the drawer or the indorsers. It is not obligatory to protect the bill; it is possible to raise an ordinary action for debt instead, but this takes longer, and without noting and protest summary diligence is unavailable.

## The effect of forgery

Forgery of a signature renders the person whose signature has been forged free from liability (BOE, s. 24). A holder in due course, who normally is well protected from other misadventures involving bills, loses his protection where there has been a forgery. However, he is protected to some extent, because an acceptor may not refuse to pay a bill on the grounds that the drawer's signature is a forgery (BOE, s. 54(2)). He will also be protected where the payee is non-existent or fictitious, since such a bill is treated as a bearer bill and can be presented for payment (BOE, s. 7(3)).

The position of cheques will be dealt with later in this chapter in the relevant section.

## Alteration

Where a bill is materially altered, without the consent of all those party to it, it becomes voidable. The person who altered it without authority will remain liable on it, as will anyone who knew of the alteration and failed to do anything about it (BOE, s. 64(1)). A holder in due course who is unaware of the alteration because it is not easily noticeable on the face of it will, however, be able to claim on the bill (BOE, s. 64(1)). Where the alteration is immaterial the bill remains valid. Immaterial alterations are such acts as crossing a cheque (BOE, s. 77) or inserting a date (BOE, s. 12).

## Discharge of bills

Bills are discharged when they are paid by the drawee or acceptor (BOE, s. 59). Where the holder and the acceptor are the same person, as may occasionally happen in commercial matters, the bill is also discharged. A bill may be renounced by the holder, who may choose not to enforce payment, but if so, this must be clearly and unconditionally expressed in writing (BOE, s. 62). A holder may also cancel a bill under BOE, s. 63.

### Prescription
Bills of exchange, cheque and promissory notes prescribe after five years, in accordance with the Prescription and Limitation (Scotland) Act 1973, s. 6(1), Sched. 1, para. 1(e).

### CHEQUES

A cheque is a bill of exchange, payable on demand, drawn on a banker (BOE, s. 73). The drawer is the person writing the cheque, the drawee is the bank; and the payee is the person to whom the money will be paid. Cheques are paid on demand, though it is possible to have a post-dated cheque. Crossing a cheque means that the funds to be paid out on the cheque may only be paid to another bank account, and the holder of the cheque cannot obtain cash. A special crossing is one where the crossing, by two parallel lines, contains the name of the bank to which payment must be made. This is rare in domestic banking. More common is a general crossing, which consists of two parallel lines and the words "A/C Payee", "Account Payee" or "Account Payee only" and in theory this requires payment to the payee's bank account only (BOE, s. 80) and makes the cheque untransferable (BOE, s. 81A(1)). If a bank does pay in cash a cheque with such a crossing on it to someone who has, say, stolen the cheque, the bank will have to reimburse the account holder and the person from whom the cheque was stolen (BOE, s. 79(2)). A cheque that is crossed "not negotiable" may be transferred, but the transferee obtains no better title than the transferor (BOE, s. 81), and could therefore lose the normal protection of being a holder in due course.

### Protection for banks
If a banker in good faith and without negligence pays a cheque into a bank account in accordance with its crossing, the banker is treated as if it had paid the cheque to the true owner of the cheque, which means that even if the cheque has been stolen the drawer's account may still be debited (BOE, s. 80) even if the cheque was not transferable in terms of BOE, s. 81A. Equally, where a bank receives a cheque for a customer and pays it into his account, and thereafter takes from the customer's account any sums due to the bank, if it transpires that the customer did not have title to the cheque, the bank will not be liable to the true owner of the cheque merely because it received payment via its customer (Cheques Act 1957, s. 4(1)). This is true even if the cheque is not transferable (Cheques Act, s. 4(2)).

In practice what normally happens with a stolen cheque is that the victim of the theft will tell the drawer to stop the cheque in order to prevent payment.

**Indorsement of cheques**

Most cheques nowadays are pre-printed with crossings already on them, thus making it difficult but not impossible to indorse cheques. Where a bank pays a cheque which is crossed but has a forged indorsement, provided it: (a) pays the cheque to another bank; (b) acted in good faith, it may debit its customer's account (BOE, s. 80).

Where a holder in due course presents an indorsed and uncrossed cheque for payment, if the banker pays out cash to the holder in good faith and in the ordinary course of business, the holder may receive payment and the drawer's account will be debited (BOE, s. 60). This is true even if the payee's indorsement has been forged, since the bank cannot be expected to check every indorsement for forgery.

**Expiry of cheques**

As a matter of banking practice and by convention, cheques are said to go "stale" after six months and will need to be re-issued.

PROMISSORY NOTES

The law relating to promissory notes may be found at BOE, ss. 83–89. A promissory note is an unconditional undertaking by one person to another, in writing, that on a fixed or determinable time he will pay a sum certain money to another person (the payee), or to someone else as instructed by the payee. Promissory notes can be negotiated in the same manner as bills of exchange, and nearly all of BOE applies to promissory notes as it does to bills of exchange, save that the provisions relating to presentment for acceptance and presentment for payment do not apply. Promissory notes may be protested and summary diligence may proceed as with bills of exchange.

**Further reading**

Chalmers and Guest, *Bills of Exchange* (15th ed., Sweet and Maxwell, 1998).
Forte (ed.), *Scots Commercial Law* (Butterworths, 1997), Chap. 5.
Gloag and Henderson, *The Law of Scotland* (10th ed., W. Green, 1995), Chap. 23.

---

# 6. INSURANCE

A contract of insurance arises where one person ("the insurer") in consideration of a payment, known as a premium, takes on the financial or other consequences ( known as risk) which amount to an uncertain event that may befall another person ("the insured") or his assets at or before a future date, certain or uncertain, whereby the insurer is required to pay money to or make good any loss to the insured on the occasion of the uncertain event.

Endowment life assurance policies are a combination of insurance and investment: the premiums that the policy holder pays are invested in such a manner that not only will the policy pay out a fixed sum on death within the predetermined period (the insurance element), but will also pay out a sum at the end of the period which is the proceeds of the invested sums and the reinvested returns on the invested premiums. In this way the assurance policy provides both protection for the insured and a savings vehicle.

**The law applicable to insurance**

Insurance is mostly governed by the common law, though the Marine Insurance Act 1906 restated and codified much of the common law in a statutory form. It is often referred to because it contains much of the best practice that insurance policies should follow. Insurance contracts are carefully worded and the insurer's liability often depends on whether the situation giving rise to a claim falls within the ambit of the words that have been chosen. Insurance is not covered by the Unfair Contract Terms Act 1977, mainly because the insurance industries' voluntary codes, the Statement of General Insurance Practice and the Statement of Long-Term Insurance Practice, cover domestic and consumer insurance practice in a manner that is effectively equivalent to what might be passed by legislation. In commercial contracts of insurance, insurers and policy holders depend on the common law and where appropriate the Marine Insurance Act 1906. Where an insurance policy combines an investment element, the Financial Services Act 1986 applies in respect of the investment element.

The insurance industry generally is regulated by the Insurance Companies Act 1982, which effectively means that insurance companies must be authorised and regulated by the DTI. The Act ensures that insurance companies maintain minimum solvency levels and are properly managed. Insurance brokers are regulated by the Insurance Brokers (Registration) Act 1977 and the Financial Services Act 1986.

Complaints about the non-investment business of insurance companies may be dealt with by the Insurance Ombudsman Bureau of which nearly all the British insurance companies are members. Complaints about the investment side of the insurance industry are dealt with by the Personal Investment Authority Ombudsman.

Life assurance policies may be written in trust for the family of the insured (Married Women's Policies of Assurance (Scotland) Act 1880).

**The terms of the insurance contract**

In order to effect an insurance contract, the person who wants to have the benefit of the insurance policy, the proposer, completes a proposal form issued by the insurance company (the insurer as above). The proposal forms, which are commonly standardised, outline the terms on which insurance companies do business. The proposer's completion of the proposal form is an offer to the insurance company, which it can accept or reject depending on the information given. Typically the insurance company will conditionally accept the offer, subject to payment of the first premium and clarification of any outstanding points. Once the proposer's proposal is accepted, and an insurance policy issued by the insurance company, the proposer becomes known as the "policyholder". The period of insurance usually starts from acceptance of payment of the first premium , though exceptionally it may start beforehand if agreed between the parties. There is no liability if there is no contract (in *Canning v. Farquhar* (1886), Canning fell off a cliff; his first premium had been tendered but not accepted, and without acceptance of the premium there was no contract).

## *Uberrimae fidei* and the duty of disclosure

The principle on which insurance proposals operate is that of *uberrimae fidei*, this meaning "the utmost good faith". So if a proposal form asks a question, it must be answered truthfully and fully and all material facts must be disclosed. In *The Spathari* (1925), the proposer deliberately concealed the underlying Greek ownership of a ship, thus breaching his duty of good faith. "Material" is defined in the Marine Insurance Act 1906, s. 12(2): "Every circumstance is material which would influence the judgment of a prudent insurer in fixing the premium or determining whether he will take the risk."

The duty of utmost good faith means that it is not enough for the proposer to rely on the phrase "to the best of my knowledge and belief" where a little research or common sense might disclose information which would be material to the insurer (in *McPhee v. Royal Insurance Co. Ltd* (1979), the proposer provided second-hand and inaccurate measurements of a boat).

Further material matters that need to be disclosed often include previous convictions (unless they are deemed to be spent under the Rehabilitation of Offenders Act 1974), the occupation of the insured, any dangerous hobbies of the insured, previous losses which were the subject of a claim and the state of the insured's health.

Matters which generally are not considered material are: such matters as diminish the insurer's risk; facts that are deemed to be common knowledge; facts about the law; facts which the insurance company checks for itself; and facts that would not be relevant to a claim. Sometimes there is doubt as to whether or not something is material, and it would appear that in England the test of materiality is that of the reasonable insurer, but in Scotland, in the context of life assurance only, the test is that of the reasonable insured (*Life Association of Scotland v. Foster* (1873), affirmed in *Hooper v. Royal London General Insurance Co. Ltd* (1993)). As regards non-life assurance, the test would appear to be that of the reasonable insurer (*Hooper*).

## Continuing duty of disclosure

Although in general there is no continuing duty of disclosure, if the insurance contract states that a material change in circumstances must be disclosed to the insurer, that must indeed be done or the policy will fall. In any case, each time the policy renewal notice appears with a request for a new payment of the premium, there is a new contract formed, albeit on the same basis as before, so that the duty to disclose arises on each occasion of the renewal of the policy.

It is a disputed question whether disclosure to an agent amounts to disclosure to the insurance company. It would appear that where the proposer has disclosed information to an agent in good faith and without intention to defraud, the insurer will be liable where the agent deceived the insurance company, as in *Bawden v. London, Edinburgh and Glasgow Assurance Co.* (1892). This can be contrasted with another case, *Newsholme Bros v. Road Transport and General Insurance Co. Ltd* (1929), where the agent inserted inaccurate information on the proposal form. The proposer knew of this but signed it anyway. The agent was held in this case to have acted for the insured person and not for the insurance company, and the insurance company was able to avoid the contract for misrepresentation.

**Warranties**
A warranty is: (a) a form of promise by the insured that a certain act will be done, or continue to be done, or as the case may be, will not be done, or that some condition will be fulfilled; or (b) a confirmation that a particular state of fact exists or does not exist. Warranties about the past do not carry forward to the future unless the wording says otherwise. Warranties do not need to be material: they need to be defined as warranties, and if the insured does not carry out the undertaking in the warranty, or if the state of affairs referred to in a warranty about the past did not take place in the manner stated, the insurer incurs no further liability with effect from the date of the breach of the warranty (Marine Insurance Act 1906, s. 33(3)).

The effect of a warranty may be seen in *Dawsons Ltd v. Bonnin* (1922), where a proposer warranted on a proposal form that a lorry was kept in a garage in central Glasgow. The lorry was later burnt in a fire in a garage elsewhere in Glasgow, and it was held that the breach of the warranty avoided the contract. It does not matter how material the warranty may be: what is significant is whether or not the warranty has been carried out, has been or is being observed or is or was correct. So if a clause is described as a warranty, it must be observed to the letter.

**The *contra proferentum* rule and the wording of contracts generally**
The rule in insurance contracts is that the meaning of the words used in such contracts is their normal everyday meaning, unless there is clear indication that some other technical meaning is used instead. If there is ambiguity in the contract, and the insurance company is trying to rely on the ambiguity of the wording of the contract to avoid liability, the construction of the wording will be interpreted contrary to the interest of the insurance company that drew up the contract. As a matter of practice, insurance contracts have gradually become easier to understand, partly through the influence of such bodies as the Plain English Campaign, partly through the *contra proferentum* rule, and partly because of the inadequate wording of earlier contracts which resulted in liability for the insurance company. In *Harris v. Poland* (1941), an elderly lady had taken out insurance for "loss" of her jewels "by fire". Before going on holiday, she carefully hid her jewels in some old newspaper and under some unlit coal in her grate. On her return she felt cold and absentmindedly lit the fire, thus damaging her jewels. She claimed for the loss by fire of her jewels and was duly successful. Had the policy said "self-induced loss" the insurer would not have been liable.

But where the wording is clear, and the insured fails to do what he is supposed to do, such as intimate a claim in time, or take reasonable precautions, there is no liability.

## Insurable interest
Since the passing of the Life Assurance Act 1774, the insured must have an insurable interest in the thing or person insured, and the interest must be a genuine family, business or other close connection. There must be a genuine insurable interest held by the insured in insured property: in *MacAura v. Northern Assurance Property Ltd* (1925), MacAura insured in his own name growing timber which was actually owned by a limited company. When it burnt down, he claimed the insurance proceeds in his own name, but was refused because the timber was owned by the company and he personally had no insurable interest in the growing timber.

## Causation
The peril that is insured against must be the proximate cause of the loss giving rise to the claim. In *Leyland Shipping Co. Ltd v. Norwich Union Fire Insurance Society* (1918), a marine policy excluded liability relating to damage from enemy action. An insured ship was torpedoed by a German submarine and was towed to Le Havre. It was not allowed to berth there lest it sank and blocked the harbour. It was towed to a spot outside the harbour where it later grounded and sank. The insurers did not have to pay out on the grounds that the proximate cause was the torpedoing by the enemy, not the grounding.

## Miscellaneous terms in insurance policies
In an indemnity policy the policy holder may not make a profit on the claim: he should recover his loss and no more. But it is possible to contract that in the event of a specified event happening, the value of which may be hard to estimate in advance, an agreed sum will be paid out for a total loss, even if in fact this may be more or less than the actual value of the loss. This is known as an *agreed value policy*.

A *reinstatement value policy* is one where the policy pays out enough to reinstate the property to the condition it was in before the insured event happened. Some property insurance policies sold in conjunction with standard securities insist that the proceeds of the policy must be used to restore the property.

A *"new for old" policy* does not aim merely to give the value of the asset as at the date of its destruction, but the value of a new asset of the same type. The premiums are correspondingly higher than for an ordinary replacement policy.

An *excess clause* requires the policy holder to pay, say, the first £100 of a claim. This discourages frivolous claims and may enable the policy holder better to retain a *no-claims bonus*, whereby the cost of the premiums diminish the longer the holder goes without having a claim.

*Over-insurance* is where an insured is paying premiums for a higher rate of insurance than the insured property is worth, perhaps because the property has depreciated. In the event of loss, it is the actual extent of the loss that will be paid, and the insured will have effectively been wasting his money by over-insuring. *Under-insurance* is where an asset is insured for less than its true worth, often because the cost of the premiums is too high for the policy holder. When a claim takes place, the insurer only pays out to the value of the sum insured, which may be much less than the value of the asset. Average is the term for the calculation of the extent of the insurer's liability in the event of under-insurance. If an asset is valued at £20,000 but is insured for £16,000, and £8,000 worth of damage occurs, the insurance company pays a proportion of the loss: in this case it would pay sixteen-twentieths of £8,000, being £6,400. The balance must be found by the owner.

*Contribution* occurs where there is more than one insurer for the same asset. Unless the terms of the insurance policies are identical this can result in long and complicated battles over liability.

*Subrogation* arises where an insured is potentially able to claim both from an insurer and from the person who caused him damage, as in a car accident. Where an insurer pays an insured following an accident, the insurer can then step into the shoes, as it were, of the insured to recoup its loss from the other driver (or his insurance company).

*Assignation* of policies is a normal procedure whereby the benefit to the proceeds of a life policy are transferred to someone else. Assignation must be accompanied in Scotland by intimation to the insurance company (Transmission of Moveable Property (Scotland) Act 1862).

*Third-party* insurance arises mostly in the context of vehicle insurance where it is compulsory (Road Traffic Act 1972, s. 143). Third-party insurance covers damage to other vehicles or people, whereas first-party insurance merely covers damage to yourself or your vehicle.

There are other occasions where insurance is compulsory: for example employers (other than the Government and local authorities) must be insured under the Employers' Liability (Compulsory Insurance) Act 1969, and solicitors have to be signed up to the Master Policy, organised by the Law Society of Scotland.

Some drivers, illegally, drive when they are not insured. If they cause an accident, the Motor Insurance Bureau, a body set up by the main insurance companies, acts as their insurance company and may pay out any claims made by victims of accidents involving uninsured drivers.

**Further reading**
Birds, *Modern Insurance Law* (4th ed., Sweet and Maxwell, 1998).
Forte (ed.), *Scots Commercial Law* (Butterworths, 1997), Chap. 4.
Gloag and Henderson, *The Law of Scotland* (10th ed., W. Green, 1995), Chap. 24.

---

# 7. AGENCY

An agent is a person who acts on behalf of a principal, bringing him into a legal relationship with a third party, but without himself necessarily being involved in that relationship. In effect there are two contracts in agency, one between the agent and the principal, and one between the principal and the third party. Common types of agent are estate agents, brokers of various kinds (stock, mortgages, insurance, ships, etc.), solicitors, publishers' agents, etc. Normally, but not exclusively, the agent is rewarded by means of a commission or fee from the principal.

An agent who by convention is given a broad area of authority to act on behalf of the principal (such as a solicitor), is known as a "general" agent, while one who is given specific instructions for a specific purpose only is known as a "special" agent (such as a travel agent). Where a special agent steps beyond the remit given to him by his principal, the principal will not in general be liable to those who deal with the special agent in areas beyond his remit.

CONSTITUTION OF AGENCY

There are different ways in which an agency may be set up, but the main ways are:

(a)  agency by express appointment;
(b)  agency by implied appointment;
(c)  agency by ratification;
(d)  agency by necessity;
(e)  agency by holding out;
(f)  *del credere* agency.

The parties to a contract of agency must have legal capacity and must exist. Where the principal does not exist, but legal obligations arise, as in a contract made by a director of an as yet unformed company, the purported agent (in this case the purported director) will himself be liable for the obligations arising out of the contract (*Phonogram Ltd v. Lane* (1982)), unless the contract says otherwise (see the Companies Act 1985, s. 36C).

Agency need not be constituted in writing, though commercial agents are entitled to obtain from their principals, and principals from their agents, a statement of the terms on which they will do business with each other (Commercial Agents (Council Directive) Regulations 1993, reg. 13).

**Agency by express appointment**
The deliberate appointment of an agent by a principal, and the grant of authority to act on the principal's behalf, whether constituted by written contract or not, is known as agency by *express appointment*.

**Agency by implication**
An agency may arise through the actings of the parties, even though there has been no express appointment (see *Barnetson v. Peterson Brothers* (1902), where a shipmaster was held entitled to act as agent for the shipowners). Agency may also be implied by operation of law: for example, a partner acts as agent for his partnership (Partnership Act 1890, s. 5).

**Agency by ratification**

The agency agreement need not pre-date the agent's actions: an agent might carry out an act for a principal who was unaware that the agent had acted for him, but on the principal's awareness of the act, the principal may ratify (*i.e.* retrospectively authorise) the act, either by a positive action or by his conduct. Three conditions, other than the legality of the contract, are required for ratification:

(a)   the agent must act as agent, and must have intimated to the third party that he was acting as agent, as in *Keighley Maxsted & Co. v. Durant* (1901) (the agent failed to reveal to the third party that he was acting as an agent and the principal was thereby unable to adopt the contract he had set up);

(b)   the principal must exist (as in *Phonogram v. Lane*, above);

(c)   the principal must have the requisite legal capacity, so that a contract struck at by the Age of Legal Capacity (Scotland) Act 1991 would not be binding on a child.

It has been argued that timeous ratification is also a condition of ratification, but there are contrary decisions on this issue both in Scotland and in England and the position remains unclear.

**Agency of necessity**

An agency of necessity arises where an agent carries out vital acts for a principal without receiving instructions. This is also known as *negotiorum gestio*. With the advent of satellite communication it is now rare for agencies of necessity to arise except in extreme climatic conditions or in a state of war. It occasionally arises where people are too ill to issue instructions, so that others are forced to act on their behalf (see *Fernie v. Robertson* (1871), where a senile person's estate was liable for house repair bills contracted on her behalf by an agent of necessity).

**Agency by holding out**

This arises either when a principal takes no steps to contradict the impression that an individual is his agent or positively encourages that impression (see *Freeman & Lockyer v. Buckhurst Park Properties (Mangal) Ltd* (1964), where a company took no steps to reverse the impression that one of its directors was authorised to act on its behalf).

***Del credere* agency**

A *del credere* agency is one where the agent guarantees payment or performance by the third party. The agent effectively bears the risk of the transaction.

THE LIABILITY OF THE PRINCIPAL FOR THE AGENT'S ACTINGS

Normally an agent will act within the limits of the authority imposed on him by his principal and the principal will therefore be liable for the agent's actings, as he also will be if he ratifies the agent's actings. However, occasionally an agent will overstep those limits, sometimes in the perceived best interests of the principal, or sometimes fraudulently. In *Panorama Developments (Guildford) Ltd v. Fidelis Furnishings Fabric Ltd* (1971), a company secretary hired cars from a car hire company apparently as part of his duties. The company was held liable for his car-hire bills, even though he had in fact used the cars on private business.

Where an agent: (a) exceeds his authority; but (b) acts in such a way that a third party has no reason to suspect that the agent is exceeding his authority; and (c) the principal has not intimated the agent's lack of authority to the third party, the principal may be liable for the agent's unauthorised act. In *Watteau v. Fenwick* (1893), where a public house manager bought cigars from a salesman despite express instructions not to do so; his employers were still liable for the cigars because the salesman was unaware that the manager did not have the requisite authority. This case has been much criticised, but it is authority for the proposition that the principal may not rely on a limitation of authority that is not communicated to a third party.

### Apparent or ostensible authority
This arises where a principal suffers a state of affairs to exist or a course of dealing to be perpetuated which gives the outside world the impression that the agent has the general authority to act as he has done, even when in fact there was no authority given for a particular unauthorised act (see *International Sponge Importers Ltd v. Watt & Sons* (1911), where a salesman had been permitted by his principal to receive payments in his own name, and the contrasting case of *British Bata Shoe Co. Ltd v. Double M. Shah Ltd* (1980), where the employer had no knowledge of the employee's actions). It also arises where an agent performs actions which are appropriate for his position (as in *Panorama v. Fidelis* and *Watteau v. Fenwick* above).

When a partner leaves a firm his former partners should strictly speaking announce his departure so that the firm can no longer be liable for his actions (Partnership Act 1890, s. 36).

### Duties of a principal to his agent
A principal is required to remunerate his agent properly and, in the absence of any express agreement, at a reasonable rate for the work involved (Commercial Agents (Council Directives) Regulations 1993). The contract of agency should clearly specify the conditions under which remuneration will be payable (see *Menzies, Bruce-Low and Thomson v. McLennan* (1895), where commission was to be payable to agents on sale of a brewery: the sale took place, but the price was not paid; the agents were nonetheless entitled to their commission).

If an agency is to be a sole agency it should say so (*Lothian v. Jenolite Ltd* (1969)). If an agent is not paid when he should be, or his expenses are not refunded, he has a right of lien over any asset of the principal's which he may have in his hands (*Glendinning v. Hope & Co.* (1912)).

Where an agent sets up a contract between his named and disclosed principal and a third party, the agent is not party to the contract and is not liable on it (*Stone & Rolfe Ltd v. Kimber Coal Co. Ltd* (1926)), unless the parties contract otherwise, as for example in a *del credere* agency. Where there is an undisclosed principal, but the principal is nonetheless identifiable, the same principle applies (*Armour v. T. L. Duff & Co.* (1912)).

Where the principal is undisclosed but the agent acts under the principal's express authority, the agent may be liable where he refuses to reveal the principal. This is because without this rule the third party would have no remedy against anyone. Accordingly under these particular circumstances the agent will be liable (*Gibb v. Cunningham & Robertson* (1925)). Where the agent is acting as an apparent principal, though in reality for an undisclosed principal, the agent is liable unless the third party discovers who the real principal is, in which case he is entitled to elect to sue either the agent or the principal (Bell, *Commentaries*, I, 540).

### Duties and liabilities of the agent

The agent is required to adhere to the terms of the contract between him and the principal. If he fails to carry out instructions he will be liable. In *Bertram Armstrong v. Godfrey (1830)*, the agent failed to sell shares at a certain high price. He waited, hoping to get an even better price. Thereupon the market crashed. The agent was held liable for the principal's loss. If the agent fails to exercise skill and care he will be liable. In *Luxmore-May v. Messenger May Baverstock* (1990), an auctioneer severely undervalued what turned out to be a masterpiece and was held liable to the original owner for the difference between the valuation and the true value.

In general an agent is only liable to the person with whom he is in a contractual relationship. In *Caparo Industries plc v. Dickman* (1990), investing shareholders relied on an inaccurate audit, as a result of which they lost a substantial sum of money attempting a takeover. It was held that the auditors were liable to the company as a whole, not to individual shareholders.

### Fiduciary duty

The principal duty of an agent to his principal is known as his *fiduciary* duty. This is the duty to act in good faith in the best interests of the principal, without letting any conflict of interest arise except insofar as it is permitted by the principal.

In *Boston Deep Sea Fishing Co. Ltd v. Ansell* (1888), Ansell, a director of the plaintiff company, failed to reveal to the plaintiffs that he had been given a secret commission for placing certain business with a firm of shipwrights. He was required to repay it to his company.

In *McPherson's Trustees v. Watt* (1877), Watt, a lawyer in Aberdeen, had been asked to deal with McPherson's estate on his death. Watt arranged for the transfer of some of McPherson's property to Watt's brother and ultimately to himself, thus allowing a conflict of duty and interest to arise. The dispositions were accordingly reduced.

In conflict of interest cases, the only cure, apart from not letting it arise, is for the agent fully to disclose his interest and seek the consent of the principal for his course of action. A further part of the fiduciary duty is that an agent is not permitted to delegate his tasks without the permission of the principal. This derives from the Roman law rule *Delegatus non potest delegare.* There are derogations from this in practice, such as when a solicitor delegates the conveyancing of a property to an assistant, though he will nonetheless be responsible for the assistant's work.

An agent is under a duty to account to his principal for all his transactions on behalf of the principal. All matters pertaining to the principal must be disclosed to him.

**Breach of warranty**

In *Anderson v. Croall & Sons Ltd* (1903), a firm of auctioneers sold, by mistake, a horse which they had no authority to sell. The purchaser, knowing that he got a bargain, demanded that he either be given the horse (which the true owner would not release) or damages, rather than merely getting his money back. It was held that the auctioneers had breached their warranty of authority to sell, and accordingly were found liable in damages to the extent of most of the true value of the horse. Their offer of a refund of the purchase price was also accepted.

TERMINATION OF AGENCY

Agency terminates by various means, including: (a) an express provision in the contract of agency; (b) the death or insanity of either the principal or agent; (c) the bankruptcy or liquidation of the principal.

If a principal wishes to ensure that he cannot possibly be liable for the actings of his agent, in an ideal world he intimates to all his customers that the agent is no longer his agent. In a large commercial organisation this is clearly impossible, and making public announcements about the termination of agencies may give customers the wrong impression. A further alternative, still often used in partnerships, is to publish a notice in the *Edinburgh Gazette* intimating that a former partner is no longer a partner of the firm.

**Further reading**

Forte (ed.), *Scots Commercial Law* (Butterworths, 1997), Chap. 8.

Gloag and Henderson, *The Law of Scotland* (10th ed., W. Green, 1995), Chap. 22.

Goode, *Commercial Law* (2nd ed., Penguin, 1995), Chap. 5.

McEwan, "Agency" in *Stair Memorial Encyclopedia* (Law Society of Scotland/Butterworths, 1987), Vol. 1.

---

# 8. PARTNERSHIP

Partnership is defined in the Partnership Act 1890, s. 1 as "the relation which subsists between persons carrying on a business in common with a view of profit". "Persons" covers all legal personae, including companies (but excluding those persons who are incapax or subject to non-age), so that it is possible for two limited companies to join together in a partnership (sometimes known as a joint venture), or for a limited company and an individual together to be a partnership. The word "firm" in the Partnership Act 1890 ("PA") means a partnership, and the name under which the partnership practises is known as the firm name. The choice of firm name must not be contrary to the provisions of the Business Names Act 1985. A list of the partners' names must be available at its place of business.

The persons involved in a partnership must be carrying on a business, so that a mere association for social purposes, such as, say, a bowling club or a dramatic society, does not qualify as a partnership.

The business must be in common. This means that where one person performs one activity, and another a different and unconnected activity, it is unlikely that they would be treated as a partnership.

Finally the partners must be operating with "a view of profit". This does not say that the partnership must make a profit; it must merely intend to do so.

### The separate legal personality of a partnership

In Scotland a firm has a separate legal personality in its own right (PA, s. 4(2)). In practice this makes little difference to the liability of the partners. A partnership may not own heritage in its own right, but has to have trustees to act for it (PA, s. 20(2)), these being the partners.

The law of partnership is derived from the old common law, and the PA codified and standardised what had generally been understood to be the law relating to partnerships. The PA established a number of standard and widely accepted rules that apply to all partnerships, while leaving it open to individual partnerships to have other terms if they wish to do so. Many partnerships are not formally set up by means of a partnership agreement, and in these cases, the PA gives guidelines to ascertain whether there is a partnership at all, to clarify what happens on the termination of the partnership, and how to divide the profits and losses between the partners. The PA is also useful where the partnership agreement is silent on any particular point.

Under the Companies Act 1985, s. 716, certain partnerships are required to incorporate once there are more than 20 partners. This rule is waived for certain professions such as doctors, accountants, lawyers, etc. (see the various Partnerships (Unrestricted Size) Regulations). As this rule is causing certain commercial difficulties, this matter is being reconsidered by the Government.

### The advantages and disadvantages of partnership

There are certain advantages and disadvantages to partnership, these being discussed at the beginning of the chapter on companies, to which reference should be made.

### Limited partnerships

These are regulated by the Limited Partnership Act 1907, and form a cross-breed between a limited company and a partnership. They are sometimes used in the farming world as a method of avoiding some of the effects of the legislation giving security of tenure to tenant farmers. They are registered in the same manner as limited companies, though under their own legislation.

In a limited partnership there is a limited partner, who contributes capital, whose liability to the partnership is limited to that amount of capital and no more (s. 4(2)), but who takes no part at all in the management on pain of becoming personally liable (s. 6(1)); and there is the general partner who bears all the risk (s. 4(2)) and depending on the terms of the partnership agreement obtains a certain amount of the profit less the sums due to the limited partner. A method of limiting the severity of the risk on either the limited or the general partner is for either partner to be a limited company.

What follows is an analysis of the Partnership Act 1890, to which reference should be made.

## RULES FOR DETERMINING THE EXISTENCE OF A PARTNERSHIP

The significance of being a partner is that not only is a partner normally entitled to the partnership's profits, but he will also be liable for the partnership's losses. It will therefore be in some persons' interests to claim that they are not partners, and hence not liable for losses, when in reality they should be liable. In the absence of a partnership agreement setting out the terms and conditions of a partnership, the following criteria, as delineated in PA, s. 2, are used to establish the existence of a partnership:

(a) joint tenancy or joint ownership, irrespective of any profits engendered by the joint tenancy or ownership, does not of itself mean that a partnership is in existence (PA, s. 2(1));

(b) the sharing of gross returns (as opposed to profits and losses), even out of any common property, does not of itself mean that a partnership is in existence (PA, s. 2(2));

(c) the receipt by a person of a share of the profits of a business is prima facie evidence that that person is a partner in the business. This means that the law presupposes that if a person receives a share of the profits he will be a partner. This presupposition may be overturned if other facts show that the person is not to be treated as a partner. Furthermore the PA states that mere receipt of a share of the profits does not automatically mean in every circumstance that the recipient is a partner. The PA, s. 2(3) gives five instances where receipt of a share of the profits does not make the recipient a partner, these being:

(i) the repayment of a debt out of the profits of a business (PA, s. 2(3)(a));

(ii) where an employee is rewarded by a share of the profits (PA, s. 2(3)(b));

(iii) where the recipient is a dependent of a former partner and receiving by way of an annuity a portion of the business's profits (PA, s. 2(3)(c));

(iv) where a lender lends money to a business and the contract for the loan, which must be in writing and signed by all the parties thereto, states that the interest rate is to vary according to the business's profits (PA, s. 2(3)(d)); and

(v) where the recipient is paid an annuity or receives some other benefit out of the profits of the business in consideration of the sale by him of the goodwill of the business (PA, s. 2(3)(e)).

As an adjunct to the above, where a person lends money to a business, or where he sells the goodwill of a business to another business, in either case expecting to receive a share of the profits but without necessarily being deemed to be a partner, if the business goes bankrupt, the lender or the seller of the goodwill, as the case may be, will find that he is treated as a postponed creditor if the borrowing or purchasing business goes into bankruptcy or other form of insolvency. Only once the other creditors have been repaid in full may the lender/seller be repaid (PA, s. 3).

## RELATIONS OF PARTNERS TO PERSONS DEALING WITH THEM

### Liability for partners' acts

Each partner is an agent for the firm, and providing the partner is acting in the usual course of business that his firm practises, his actions bind the firm (PA, s. 5). Where the partner does not in fact have the authority to act in a particular transaction, and the person with whom he is dealing either knows that the partner does not have authority for the transaction, or does not know or believe that the partner is a partner, the transaction will not bind the partnership.

This raises the issue of actual and apparent authority, and the extent of the knowledge of the person with whom the partner is dealing. The assumption is that when a partner signs a document on behalf of the partnership he will bind the partnership (PA, s. 6), even if as a matter of practice his fellow partners have not permitted him to do so (see *Mercantile Credit Co. Ltd v. Garrod* (1962), where an unauthorised partner sold a car contrary to his partnership agreement, and the firm was held bound by his action), unless the matter has been specifically brought to the attention of the contracting party (PA, s. 8). If the contracting party's belief in the authority of the partner was unjustified, the partnership will also not be bound (see *Paterson Bros v. Gladstone* (1891), where borrowing by one partner, ostensibly on partnership business, of money at an interest rate of 40 per cent could not be construed as acting in the normal course of business). In *Fortune v. Young* (1918), a partner guaranteed the financial standing of a young man seeking a tenancy. This was written on partnership headed paper, but it was held that this was clearly a private matter outwith partnership business and the firm was not bound by the letter.

Should a partnership be sued and be unable to meet a decree, technically the debt should be satisfied out of the partnership assets first, and thereafter by the individual partners personally. However, PA, s. 4(2) states that where there is a decree against a firm, or diligence could be levelled against a firm, the creditor may proceed directly against any partner he chooses who is entitled to relief *pro rata* from the firm and the other partners. Partners in a firm are jointly and severally liable for the debts of the firm arising while they are partners: if they die while still partners, their estate then becomes liable in their stead (PA, s. 9).

## Non-partners may bind the firm in contracts

It is not necessary to be a partner to bind a partnership to a contract. Under PA, s. 6 anyone with apparent authority to bind the partnership may do so.

## Misappropriation of property by partners

Where an individual partner, or the whole firm, in each case apparently acting within the course of his or its business, receives money from a third party and misapplies it, the firm is liable for the loss (PA, s. 11). However, if an individual partner, acting as a trustee, improperly misuses trust property in the firm's business or on account of the partnership, he alone of the partners remains liable for the misapplied property, though any other partner who is aware of the breach by the partner/trustee may still be liable if he has been notified of the partner/trustee's breach, and the property itself may still be recovered from the partnership if it is still in its hands (PA, s. 13).

## Holding out persons as partners

Where someone purports to be a partner even when he is not, or where a partnership "holds out" or does not contradict the impression that someone is a partner even when he is not, the partnership as a whole will be liable to anyone who lends money to the firm in the belief that the purporting partner is indeed a partner (PA, s. 14).

## Partners cannot avoid responsibility by claiming ignorance of their fellow partners' pronouncements or by claiming that they have not been informed

Any admission or representation by a partner made in the ordinary course of business about partnership matters may be evidence against the firm (PA, s. 15). This means that if a partner makes an assertion about the firm, he is deemed to have made it on all his fellow partners' behalf, and they cannot pretend to be ignorant of it or assert that his statement was not binding on them.

The converse of section 15 is that a notice to any one partner about any partnership matter is deemed to be notice to the firm as a whole, so that other partners cannot claim that they were ignorant of a matter merely because one of their fellows had failed to communicate the matter to them (PA, s. 16).

## Vicarious liability of partners

The firm is vicariously liable for any wrongful act or omission of a partner in the ordinary course of business and which causes injury to a non-partner (PA, s. 10). However, where one partner injures another in the course of business, as when one fisherman hurt another with a boathook in *Mair v. Wood* (1948), no liability attaches to the partnership.

## The liability of new and retiring partners

An incoming partner is not liable for any debts of the partnership arising from before he became a partner (PA, s. 17(1)); a retiring partner remains liable for the debts arising during the period of his partnership (PA, s. 17(2)). Normally when a partner retires, the terms of his retiral will clarify what continuing liabilities he will remain responsible for, though as far as outsiders are concerned the retired partner is still liable for the debts arising during his period of partnership. Where a retiring partner has not properly notified third parties of his retirement, he may still be liable as if he were still a partner (PA, s. 36(1)), but notice in the *Edinburgh Gazette* serves as notice of retiral to those who have not had dealings with the firm. It does not, however, serve as notice to those who have had dealings with the firm. In theory they need more formal intimation, though in practice this is rarely followed: the usual form of intimation is a change in the partners' names on the headed paper.

## THE RELATIONS OF PARTNERS TO ONE ANOTHER

As stated above it is normal and indeed sensible for prospective partners to draw up a partnership agreement. In the absence of an express agreement, agreement may be inferred from the partners' course of dealing (PA, s. 19). Partnership property is assumed to be owned by the partnership and each partner is entitled to a *pro indiviso* share, which means that while he may not be easily able to realise partnership property, and creditors cannot effect diligence on the partnership property as a whole if their claim is against the partner in his private capacity, he is entitled on the sale of the partnership property to his proportion of the sale proceeds (PA, s. 20). The PA, s. 24 outlines the normal rules that will apply to partnerships unless disapplied or varied by the partnership agreement, such as equal division of profits and losses, repayment of partnership expenses, loans to the partnership other than the contribution of partnership capital, interest on the capital, the right to share in the management of the partnership, the prohibition on remuneration for acting in the partnership business, the requirement for the consent of all partners for the adoption of a new partner, the use of the majority vote in deciding partnership business except in the context of changing the partnership business which attracts a unanimous vote, and the accessibility of the partnership books.

The PA, s. 25 states that no partner may be expelled by mere majority of votes unless the partnership agreement permits this, and section 26 permits retirement at will, subject to any agreement to the contrary.

There is a duty on all partners to render proper and true accounts and to provide true information to each other (PA, s. 28). Partners must account to the partnership for any profit deriving from the partnership (PA, s. 29) and no partner may compete with his firm (PA, s. 30). In *Pillans Bros v. Pillans* (1908), one of the brothers and partners in a family firm of manufacturers set up a rival business not far from his family firm. He was required to account to the family firm for his profits from the business. Where a partner assigns his interest in the firm to a third party, the third party has no right of management of that partner's share of the business; instead it merely entitles the assignee to the share of the profits (PA, s. 31). It is common for a partnership agreement to prohibit assignation without the consent of the other partners.

## DISSOLUTION OF THE PARTNERSHIP

A partnership is dissolved either by the means specified in the partnership agreement, or in the absence of a partnership agreement, by one of the methods stated in the PA, s. 32, these being the expiry of a designated term, the completion of the undertaking for which the partnership was set up, or by one partner giving notice to the other of his intention to dissolve the partnership. The death or bankruptcy of any partner may also cause the partnership to be dissolved (PA, s. 33) unless the partnership agreement says otherwise. Equally, should the partnership be carrying on an illegal activity, it will be dissolved (PA, s. 34). The court may dissolve the partnership if the partnership cannot be dissolved by any consensual method, under the PA, s. 35, in particular on the occasion of the insanity of a partner, the permanent incapacity of a partner, the misconduct of a partner such that his misconduct would materially affect the carrying out of the partnership business, breach of the partnership business such that the other partners cannot practicably carry on business with him, the partnership making a loss, or where the court considers it just and equitable to dissolve the partnership. Notwithstanding dissolution, the partners remain liable for the debts of the partnership until creditors have been informed of the dissolution of the partnership (PA, s. 36), so it is in the partners' interests to notify the dissolution of the partnership as soon as possible: there are mechanisms to permit this (PA, s. 37). The partners retain some rights to deal with the partnership property even after the dissolution of the partnership, but only for the purpose of winding up the affairs for the partnership (PA, s. 38). The partnership assets are sold or otherwise used to pay the partnership debts, but any surplus remaining after repayment of creditors is divided between the partners on the basis outlined in the partnership agreement or such other basis as may be agreed (PA, s. 39). Where the partnership has been dissolved because of the fraud of one or more of the partners, the innocent partner (or partners) is entitled to redress from the fraudulent partners (PA, s. 41), and is thereby entitled to a lien over the partnership assets as a method of ensuring his ultimate payment of the sums properly due to him. He is also entitled to be indemnified by the fraudulent partner for any liabilities of the partnership incurred by the fraudulent partner but which had to be paid by the partnership or the innocent partner.

Where a partner dies or retires and the partnership business continues for a while after dissolution as part of the winding up of the partnership, the dead partner's estate or the retiring partner is entitled to his share of the profits or to interest at 5 per cent, unless there is an option available to other partners to buy the dead or retired partners' share (PA, s. 42).

Once the partnership assets have been realised, the partnership debts are repaid, first to creditors, then to each partner in respect of advances, next to each partner in respect of his capital and finally the balance is divided up between the partners in the same proportion as profits have been divided up (PA, s. 44).

If the partnership becomes insolvent, the Bankruptcy (Scotland) Act 1985 applies to its winding up.

**Further reading**

Forte (ed.), *Scots Commercial Law* (Butterworths, 1997), Chap. 9.

Gloag and Henderson, *The Laws of Scotland* (10th ed., W.Green, 1995), Chap. 56.

Pearson and Tyre, "Partnership", *Stair Memorial Encyclopedia* (Law Society of Scotland/Butterworths, 1995), Vol. 16.

---

# 9. COMPANY LAW

## The comparative advantage of the limited company

The major drawback of being a sole trader is his unlimited liability for his debts, and the risk of bankruptcy if his business fails to prosper.

The benefits of being a partner in a partnership are:

(a) colleagues with whom to share losses as well as profits;

(b) the ease and informality of setting up a partnership;

(c) rights of management in the partnership;

(d) privacy in respect of the partnership's accounts;

(e) the absence of any requirement to produce audited accounts; and

(f) freedom to practise any trade or business the partnership wishes;

all subject to any agreement between the partners otherwise.

The disadvantages are:

(a) the risk of unlimited liability for the partnership's debts;

(b) the difficulty of raising a loan against the value of any assets other than heritage;

(c) the requirement that partnerships with more than 20 partners must incorporate (with certain exceptions for professional persons such as doctors, solicitors, etc.).

These two forms of trading may be contrasted with trading through a registered company, the advantages of which are as follows:

(a) companies have a legal personality separate from those who are employed by it, those who manage it and those who own it;

(b) there is no restriction on the maximum number of members a company may have, though public companies must have a minimum of two, and private companies a minimum of one member;

(c) it is possible to be a member of a company without having to be involved in the management of a company;

(d) a member is not normally liable for the debts of a company beyond the fully paid up value of each share and any premium on the share, unless:

(i) the member has by a separate undertaking guaranteed the company's debts;

(ii) the company is a guarantee company in which case he may have to honour the guarantee;

(iii) the company is an unlimited liability company;

(iv) the member has been involved in certain fraudulent activities;

(e) companies may grant security over non-heritable assets by way of a floating charge; this enables them quickly to raise finance with which to exploit a commercial opportunity;

(f) companies may raise funds by offering their shares for sale;

(g) a successful company may offer its shares for sale to the public through a recognised investment exchange, such as the Stock Exchange, thus creating significant opportunities for wealth, both for entrepreneurs and investors;

(h) some company directors enjoy the status of being a company director;

(i) in theory a company may continue indefinitely without ever having to be reconstituted (this being known as "perpetual succession"); even if its members and directors change, the company still remains in existence.

The disadvantages of being a limited company are:

(a) the company must disclose its accounts and other details on a regular basis — thus revealing information to competitors;

(b) most companies' accounts need to be audited at some cost and inconvenience;

(c) companies must be formed in a prescribed manner; there are costs incurred in incorporation and in complying with the requirements of company law generally;

(d) it is difficult for an investor to withdraw his capital from the company;

(e) although directors are not normally responsible for their company's debts, in certain instances, such as insolvency, the directors may find themselves liable for the company's debts despite the separate legal personality of the company;

(f) creditors of small companies often demand personal guarantees from the members or directors, thus removing one of the principal advantages of being a limited company, the freedom from liability for the company's debts.

## THE LEGISLATION APPLICABLE TO COMPANIES

Companies are regulated primarily by:

(a) Companies Act 1985 ("CA"), which incorporates substantial amendments made by the Companies Act 1989;

(b) Insolvency Act 1986 ("IA");

(c) Company Directors (Disqualification) Act 1986 ("CDDA");

(d) Business Names Act 1985 ("BNA");

(e) Financial Services Act 1986 ("FSA").

## THE SEPARATE LEGAL PERSONALITY OF A COMPANY

The separate legal personality of a company has been well established by three cases. (1) *Salomon v. A. Salomon & Co. Ltd* (1897). There was no bar to Salomon lending money to his own company and securing the loan by a floating charge. (2) *Lee v. Lee's Air Farming Ltd* (1961). The director and majority owner of the company was entitled to contract in his personal capacity as an employee with his own company. (3) *MacAura v. Northern Assurance Co. Ltd* (1925). A timber grower transferred the ownership but not the insurance policy of his timber to a limited company which he controlled. He was unable to claim on the insurance policy for the destruction of the timber, as the policy was not in favour of the company.

### Lifting the veil under common law

Although the law recognises that a company is a separate entity from its owners, managers or employees, there are occasions under common law and under statute where this principle is eroded. This is known as "lifting the veil of incorporation" and enables the court to look at the underlying details of the company. Well known cases under common law where this has arisen include:

*Daimler Co. Ltd v. Continental Tyre and Rubber Co. Ltd* (1916). In wartime, a predominantly enemy-owned company was forbidden to claim for a debt due by a British company.

*Gilford Motor Co. Ltd v. Horne* (1933). Horne could not avoid the terms of a restrictive covenant by claiming that he was working for a company which was not bound by the restrictive covenant.

*Re FG Films Ltd* (1953). It was held that a company which was British in registration but American in every other respect should be treated as if it were a foreign company and taxed accordingly.

*Re H* (1996). Customs and Excise were held entitled to treat as personal assets of the defendants the assets of two companies through which a substantial fraud had been perpetrated by the defendants.

The case of *Creasey v. Breachwood Motors Ltd* (1962), popularly cited as a new extension of the principle of lifting the veil, has been overruled in a similar case *Ord v. Belhaven Pubs Ltd* (1998).

### The corporate entity theory

Where a group of companies form an interlocking whole, it has been suggested in *DHN Food Distributors Ltd v. Tower Hamlets LBC* (1976) that a benefit payable to one of the companies, but which through a technicality was not eligible for the benefit, could be paid to another company within the group. This approach, of lumping closely connected companies within a group, was not well regarded in *Woolfson v. Strathclyde Regional Council* (1978), and in *Adam v. Cape Industries plc* (1990), the current principle was established that companies must be treated as separate from each other, unless there is evidence that a company is being used as a façade to conceal the true facts. This means that in principle holding companies have no liability for their subsidiaries.

## Lifting the corporate veil under statute

There are certain occasions under statute where the law will look at the underlying reality of the company or will treat the members or as the case may be the officers of the company as liable for the debts of the company. Some of these are as follows:

(a) IA, s. 122(1)(f) (known as the just and equitable grounds) — a quasi-partnership company was wound up following the breach of faith between former partners who had subsequently incorporated their business (*Ebrahimi v. Westbourne Galleries Ltd* (1973));

(b) CA, s. 117 — absence of trading certificate for a public company (as a matter of practice extremely rare) may make the directors personally liable for the company's debts;

(c) CA, s. 349 — inaccuracy of company name on cheque, etc., makes the signing officer personally liable (*Rafsanjan Pistachio Producers Ltd v. Reiss* (1990));

(d) CA, s. 24 — a public company with only one member for more than six months makes that member liable for his company's debts;

(e) IA, s. 213 — fraudulent trading by anyone involved with a subsequently insolvent company makes that person liable for the company's debts;

(f) IA, ss. 212, 214 — misfeasance or wrongful trading by directors of subsequently insolvent companies make them liable for the company's debts.


## TYPES OF COMPANY

The two main types of company are private companies and public companies.
    There are in turn several different types of private company:

(a) unlimited company (rarely used, for the members are personally responsible for the company's debts; no accounts need be published);
(b) guarantee company (commonly used for charities; members are liable for the company's debts up to a guaranteed amount);
(c) private limited company limited by shares (by far the most common);
(d) single member private limited company limited by shares (common for wholly owned subsidiaries and certain small businesses).

It is also possible to categorise private companies by size, so that there are small companies, medium sized companies and large companies. Certain small companies do not need to provide audited accounts. Neither small nor medium sized companies need produce full accounts.
    It is possible to convert an unlimited company into a private limited company, and indeed a private limited company into a public company.
    There is only type of public limited company. The principal features of a public company (commonly known as a "plc") are that:

(a) it has a minimum authorised capital of £50,000 and each share must be paid up to the extent of one quarter plus any premium;

(b) the company law rules relating to public companies are considerably stricter and require more disclosure of information and accounts than private companies;

(c) a public company could, if it wished, offer its shares to the public.

There is a common misconception that all public companies offer their shares to the public. Some public companies do offer their shares to the public. However, many public companies do not do so: they are merely "public" companies because the more stringent capital requirements and the words "plc" give the company more credibility and status that it might not otherwise have. However if a company does wish to offer its shares to the public, it must be a public company to do so, for private companies may not issue their shares to the public (CA, s. 81).

Companies that wish to offer their shares to the public generally do so on the Stock Exchange (in which case they are said to be "listed" on the Stock Exchange) or on some other market such as the Alternative Investment Market. In either case, the companies concerned have to comply both with the rigorous disclosure requirements of each market and with the terms of the FSA.

## CORPORATE DISCLOSURE

All companies must disclose information about themselves at the Register of Companies. Failure to send certain documents, such as accounts, to the Registrar of Companies within strict time limits may result in prosecution. Members may also find out about their companies through receiving their annual accounts and directors' reports and may attend shareholders' meetings.

### The incorporation of a company

In order to incorporate a company, a company needs to provide certain documentation for the Registrar of Companies, these being Form 10 (the initial statement of directors, shareholders, company name (which must not be contrary to BNA) and registered office), Form 12 (the statutory declaration endorsing form 10), the memorandum of association, the articles of association, and the registration fee. A company's *memorandum of association* is a public document stating amongst other things the company's name and principal trading activity. A company's *articles of association* are its internal constitution, detailing how shares may be transferred, directors appointed, meetings held, the rules attaching to different classes of shares, etc. Most companies' articles are based on a template known as *Table A*, though few companies adopt Table A in its entirety, most altering it to some extent to suit their particular requirements (see, for example, *Bushell v. Faith* (1970), where weighted voting was declared to be acceptable) providing that the alteration does not contravene any other rule of law. Companies should stay within the limits imposed on themselves by the memorandum and articles of association, and there are mechanisms to enable members of a company to force the directors to adhere to the company's own rules as laid out therein (CA, s. 35).

Equally, members, on joining a company, must accept the terms of the memorandum and articles as they form part of the effective contract between the member and the company as to the terms on which the members hold their shares in the company (CA, s. 14) (see also *Hickman v. Kent and Romney Marsh Sheepbreeders Association* (1915)). Classes of shareholders are able to protect their own interests by the rule that states that only they may vote on any change to their rights; it is not possible for non-class members to rewrite the class-members' rights (CA, s. 125). If the members generally do not like the wording of the memorandum or articles, they may change most elements within the memorandum and articles by means of a special resolution of the members (CA, ss. 4, 9).

## THE MANAGEMENT OF A COMPANY

### Directors
The company is managed by its directors. They are given authority to deal with the commercial and administrative affairs of the company (Table, art. 70), subject to some powers of management (such as dismissing the directors under CA, s. 303) being retained by the members. It is possible to be a member and a director simultaneously. As directors know better than anyone what is taking place within their company, there are extensive rules, both under common law and under statute (CA, ss. 311–347), to prevent directors taking unauthorised advantage of their position within the company to unduly benefit themselves. Directors have a fiduciary duty to work in good faith in the best interests of the company as a whole (see *Boston Deep Sea Fishing Co. Ltd v. Ansell* (1888)). Where they fail to do so, they will be required to make good any loss to the company or repay any unauthorised profit. Negligent directors have a duty of care to the company and will be required to make good any losses to the company (*Dorchester Finance Co. Ltd v. Stebbing* (1989)). Directors of insolvent companies may also be required to make good any losses to the company under IA, ss. 212–216. Under exceptional circumstances directors may be banned as directors for up to 15 years by the CDDA where their conduct as a director so merits disqualification.

### Company secretary and auditor
The *company secretary* ensures that the company complies with all its legal requirements, organises meetings, sends documents to the Registrar of Companies, takes the minutes of meetings, etc. He often is an accountant, lawyer or chartered secretary.

The *auditor* is required to check the company's accounts prior to the accounts being lodged with the Registrar of Companies. He has to make a report on the accounts which should state that the accounts present a "true and fair" view of the company's financial state.

## COMPANY BORROWINGS

A company may borrow just like any other legal person. The common name for the document outlining the terms of a loan to a company is a debenture or bond. A company may grant charges over its property as security for the loan. Such charges must be registered with the Registrar of Companies. For further details, see the chapter on security.

## SHARES

A share is a unit of ownership in a company owned by a shareholder, and is commonly designated as having a *nominal* or notional (but not market) value of £1.00. The nominal value of a share is the amount that must be paid by a shareholder to subscribe for a share from the company in order to avoid any further liability to the company. The ownership of shares is commonly evidenced by a share certificate. Shareholders are commonly entitled, amongst other things, to a dividend out of the company's profits (if declared), a right of voting at meetings, to see the accounts and directors' report, and to a return of capital on solvent liquidation of the company. It is possible for a company to have many different classes of shares, each with differing rights and obligations, so that there may be non-voting shares, preference shares, convertible shares, redeemable shares, etc.

### Shareholders' meetings

Most companies must have annual general meetings at which the directors explain the accounts and highlight the future direction of the company. The members may vote on any resolutions that require their assent. Shareholders' meetings are designed to make directors accountable to the members, although this does not always happen in practice. Nonetheless meetings form an admirable opportunity to embarrass directors who have failed to exercise their responsibilities usefully. Members may vote on resolutions, the type of resolution varying according to the significance of the issue:

(a) special resolutions require the approval of 75 per cent of the voting members and 21 days' notice: they are used for major matters relating to the capital of the company or its constitution;

(b) ordinary resolutions require a bare majority and 14 days' notice and are used for lesser matters such as removal of directors and the approval of directors' contracts;

(c) extraordinary resolutions require 75 per cent approval but only 14 days' notice and are used to put a company into voluntary liquidation or for classes of shareholders to vary their rights.

It is possible to have written and elective resolutions in private companies.

## LIQUIDATION

A liquidator is a person who is appointed either by the creditors or the members to wind up the company, in other words to sell the company's assets or otherwise turn the company's assets into cash which is then divided up between the creditors. A winding up may be either compulsorily ordered by the court (IA, s. 122) because of the company's inability to pay its debts (IA, s. 122(1)(f)) or because it would be just and equitable to do so (IA, s. 122(1)(g)), or voluntarily agreed upon by the members (IA, ss. 84–116). A members' voluntary liquidation means that the company is solvent and can pay its debts in full; a creditors' voluntary liquidation anticipates that the company is insolvent, in which case preferential creditors are paid in full first if possible, then ordinary creditors if there are sufficient funds to distribute to them. Where assets are subject to a charge, such as a standard security over heritage, or a floating charge over moveables, the liquidator is only entitled to deal with the surplus, if any, of the value of the assets over the extent of the charge. A liquidator follows substantially the same rules as does a trustee in bankruptcy and has the same powers to swell the estate by setting aside antecedent transactions, and to equalise diligence, all with a view to maximising the sums due to the creditors. It is open to him to reduce gratuitous alienations (IA, s. 242), unfair preferences (IA, s. 243), extortionate credit transactions (IA, s. 244), and certain floating charges which may have been granted in order to defraud creditors (IA, s. 245). Where directors have misapplied company assets (IA, s. 212), or where fraudulent trading (IA, s. 213), wrongful trading (IA, s. 214), or trading through a phoenix company (IA, s. 216) have been taking place, the liquidator may apply to the court to make the directors accountable to the company.

### Further reading

Gloag and Henderson, *The Law of Scotland* (10th ed., W. Green, 1995), Chap. 51.

Grier, *U.K. Company Law* (Wiley, 1998).

Keenan and Bisacre, *Company Law for Students* (10th ed., Pitmans, 1996).

Sealy, *Cases and Materials in Company Law* (6th ed., Butterworths, 1996).

---

# 10. RIGHTS IN SECURITY

A lender will seek security for a loan because by doing so he has a better chance of getting his loan back, and the interest thereon, than if he lends the money on an unsecured basis.

If, in addition to having security over a borrower's assets, the lender can have first right to the proceeds of sale of those assets, even when the borrower becomes insolvent, the lender is in an even better position. Indeed, unless he has that right, he may charge a high rate of interest, refuse to lend or, in the case of a limited company, demand extensive personal guarantees from the directors of the company.

There are two main types of security in Scots law: there are "real rights" (*jura in re*), which give the security holder a right in the secured property, and "personal rights" (*jura in personam*), which are rights against a person.

### *Jura in re*

A real right gives a creditor a right in the property itself which, generally speaking, cannot be defeated by others' interests. Even if the debtor becomes insolvent the creditor may still have a right in the property. It is better, from a creditor's point of view, to have a real right in property than a personal right against a person. This is because most items of property can usually be traced and found, whereas a person may disappear or become insolvent, thus making the pursuit of the personal right against a debtor pointless.

The type of real right depends on (a) what the property is and (b) who the debtor is. As regards (a), property in Scotland is divided into three main categories, these being: heritable property (effectively land and buildings, in England called "real estate"), also known as "heritage", and sometimes more loosely as "property"; corporeal moveable property (tangible assets that can be taken from place to place, such as vehicles and machinery); and incorporeal moveable property (shares, royalties, book debts and other items which though commonly evidenced by paper documentation have no tangible existence).

All legal personae may grant security over any of the assets in (a). As regards (b), companies registered under the Companies Acts are also able to have a further type of security that is unavailable to other legal personae, this being a floating charge, which covers not only present assets, but also future assets as they may be from time to time, and which becomes a fixed charge on the occurrence of certain events. Floating charges will be dealt with in detail later.

### The significance of delivery

Historically the Scots law on security is derived from Roman law: *traditionibus, non nudis pactis, transferuntur rerum dominia* — by delivery alone, and not by bare agreement, is the ownership in things transferred. If the asset is safely delivered into the lender's hands, there is no doubt as to the strength of the security. As this is not without its logistical problems, the law has had to come up with various ingenious stratagems to ensure that the lender's rights are preserved, even when the object of the security is physically immoveable, such as heritage, or in practical terms is bulky or difficult to identify.

### SECURITY OVER HERITAGE

As it is clearly impossible physically to deliver land, security over heritage is now effected by drawing up a contractual security document (a "standard security") between the lender and the borrower and subsequently registering it in the Register of Sasines or the Land Register. On its registration the lender obtains a real right in the heritage and becomes known as a "heritable creditor", or sometimes as a standard security holder. The law relating to standard securities is to be found in the Conveyancing and Feudal Reform (Scotland) Act 1970 ("CFRSA"), which sets out the procedure for their registration, standard styles for the wording of standard securities (Sched. 2) along with standard conditions that are incorporated into all standard securities (Sched. 3).

Such conditions provide for the right of both the heritable creditor and the property owner with regards to the maintenance of the property, the procedure for dealing with default by the debtor or property owner, the right of eviction of the property owner following the service of calling up notices or the insolvency of the property owner, the heritable creditor's right to repossess, sell or foreclose on the property, as well as the rights of the property owner to redeem his standard security and thus have it discharged. There are also provisions to ensure that the debtor or owner is treated fairly and that if any surplus arises out of the sale of the secured assets, the surplus is made over to the owner. When a heritable creditor exercises his rights under a standard security, he is not required to go to the court to obtain a court order to remove the owner, since the terms of the standard security enable him to repossess the property, though as a matter of practice many heritable creditors may choose to obtain a court order anyway.

## TENANTED PROPERTY SUBJECT TO A STANDARD SECURITY

One of the standard conditions of a standard security is the prohibition on granting a lease over secured property without the consent of the heritable creditor (Sched. 3, cond. 6). If this prohibition is contravened, the lease may be reduced by the heritable creditor, which means that the tenant may lose his tenancy on the occasion of his landlord's failure to maintain his payments to the heritable creditor. However, if a heritable creditor at the time of the creation of the standard security is already aware of an existing or intended lease, he is precluded from enforcing his rights against the tenant (*Trade Development Bank v. Warriner and Mason (Scotland) Ltd* (1980)).

Where the heritable creditor consents to the presence of tenants, and the debtor defaults, the existing leases are transferred to the heritable creditor, who may also issue new leases (Sched. 3, cond. 10(4),(5)).

### Discharge of standard security
On repayment of the loan for which the standard security was granted, or if the heritable creditor waives his rights, the standard security is discharged and the redemption of standard security registered in the same manner as the standard security.

### The advantage of the standard security
The advantage of the standard security is that it is a "fixed" charge and that it defeats all other rights. If the owner of the property is sequestrated, and any secured heritage has to be sold by the trustee in sequestration (or the heritable creditor as the case may be), the heritable creditor is entitled to the proceeds of the sale of the property in priority to all other creditors. Consequently lenders will always try to obtain a standard security over heritage whenever they can. Once a standard security is in place over heritage, it is impossible for the owner of the heritage to sell the property without first obtaining the standard security holder's consent to the discharge of the standard security — which will generally only be obtained by repayment of any loan secured over the heritage.

**Ranking of standard securities**

It is possible to have more than one standard security over the same piece of heritage. Normally the order of priority of the securities will be the date order in which they were registered, unless that order is varied by means of a ranking agreement. In the absence of a ranking agreement, when a second security holder registers his security, the first security holder has his security limited to the sums already advanced or required to be advanced in terms of the security documentation, together with interest and expenses (CFRSA, s. 13(1)). Where there are floating charges (see later), the floating charge will be postponed to any properly registered standard securities (Companies Act 1985, s. 464(3)), although it is possible for a floating charge to take precedence over a standard security where there is a clause in the floating charge prohibiting the creation of a prior-ranking fixed security (*AIB Finance Ltd v. Bank of Scotland* (1993), discussed later in the context of floating charges).

## SECURITY OVER CORPOREAL MOVEABLES

As indicated earlier, delivery or its equivalent is required for effective security. As regards moveable items, the simplest method is known as pledge, which is the physical handing over of an asset to the security holder. It may not always be physically possible to hand over the goods, so effective delivery is possible. In *West Lothian Oil Co. (in liquidation) v. Mair* (1892), barrels of oil were placed in a locked and fenced off part of a yard and the security holder given the key: this was held to be a satisfactory form of security. Constructive delivery is similar, but as indicated in *HD Pochin & Co. v. Robinows & Marjoribanks* (1869), (a) the goods must be genuinely in the hands of an independent third party, not the debtor or his agent, (b) the third party must be informed that he holds the goods on behalf of the security holder, (c) the secured goods must be ascertained and identifiable, and (d) the debtor must have no continuing right to dispose of the goods, except as the creditor's agent (*North-Western Bank Ltd v. Poynter, Son and Macdonalds* (1894)).

Symbolic delivery is permissible where the goods themselves do not easily lend themselves to unnecessary warehousing and, by convention, it is accepted that the pledge of a bill of lading is equivalent to the pledge of the goods themselves (*Hayman & Son v. McLintock* (1907)). Likewise, a mercantile agent may pledge goods using the documents of title to those goods (Factors Act 1889, s. 3).

Normally with a pledge the terms of the pledge documentation allow the creditor to sell the pledged goods, but if such a term is absent, the creditor may apply to court for warrant to sell the goods (Bell, *Principles*, s. 207).

Pawnbroking is a form of pledge and is extensively regulated by the Consumer Credit Act 1974, ss. 114–122.

## LIEN

Whereas a pledge requires the deliberate act of a pledgor willing to hand over his goods to the creditor or to a third party for the benefit of the creditor, lien is involuntary from the pledgor's point of view and arises out of the exercise of a right by the creditor who is already in possession of the goods. A solicitor's lien arises when a client fails to pay his bills. The solicitor will not release the client's papers to another solicitor until he is paid first for what he has done. The right of lien does not automatically give the creditor the right to sell the goods: an application to court would be necessary for that to take place, except (a) under the unpaid seller's lien arising from the Sale of Goods Act 1979, s. 39, whereby an unpaid seller may, after giving reasonable notice, resell goods that have not been paid for even where the property in the goods has passed to the buyer, and (b) an innkeeper's lien whereby if a guest has not paid his bill, his retained goods may be auctioned after a period of six weeks (Innkeeper's Act 1878).

HYPOTHEC

Although the basis of the law of security is that delivery to the creditor and possession by the creditor is vital, there are some occasions where on a practical basis this is not possible. Such occasions are known as hypothecs. A landlord's hypothec is a form of security for one year's worth of rent. Nowadays it is mostly used for commercial subjects, though it may be used for agricultural land not exceeding two acres in size. The landlord may retain the tenant's goods and following a particular court procedure, known as sequestration for rent, he may sell the debtor's assets. It does not normally extend to goods on the premises owned by persons other than the tenant or the tenant's assignees, though the position in this respect is far from clear (see Wilson, *The Scottish Law of Debt* (2nd ed., W. Green, 1991) and *Grampian Regional Council v. Drill Stem (Inspection Services) Ltd (in receivership)* (1994)).

It is possible to grant a security (without either delivery to or possession by the creditor) over a ship or an aircraft by means of a ship or aircraft mortgage, registrable respectively under the Merchant Shipping Act 1894 and which the Civil Aviation Authority. Companies granting such mortgages will also need to register them with the Registrar of Companies (Companies Act 1985, s. 410(4)(d)).

PSEUDO-SECURITY

**Disguised security**
One method of having a purported security is the artificial sale. An example of this is sale and lease-back, with the underlying intention being that the creditor, instead of being given a security over a moveable item, purportedly buys it from the debtor and then leases it back to the debtor, so that the lease payments cover the debtor's debt and interest. The advantage of this from the creditor's point of view is that he owns the item, which is better than a mere security. If the transaction is in reality meant to be a charge or other form of security, the Sale of Goods Act 1979, s. 62(4) states that the provisions of the Sale of Goods Act 1979 do not apply. If this is the case then the common law must apply, and ownership may only pass on delivery.

If no delivery takes place, no security may be effected. If the debtor then becomes insolvent, the creditor may then have no rights in the asset. The wording of section 62(4) is not entirely clear on this issue, and there are contradictory dicta in case law as to the true meaning (*Robertson v. Hall's Trustee* (1896), and *Gavin's Trustee v. Fraser* (1920)) depending on whether or not one takes the view (a) that the underlying intentions may be ascertained to see whether there is in reality an intention to create a security, or (b) that the written contract embodies the parties' overall intention and any underlying intentions, if not expressed, are irrelevant.

**Retention of title**
There is, however, no doubt that a retention of title clause is perfectly valid under the Sale of Goods Act 1979, ss. 17 and 19, even for all sums due from any other transactions between buyer and seller (*Armour v. Thyssen Edelstahlwerke AG* (1990)). A retention of title clause is in effect a security, though under the Sale of Goods Act 1979, s. 25, a seller's rights may be defeated by a subsequent purchaser acquiring the seller's goods in good faith, and may also be defeated if the goods are no longer identifiable.

## ASSIGNATION

Assignation is the method of effecting a security over incorporeal moveable property such as licences, royalties, copyrights, proceeds of an insurance policy, rents, book debts, etc. The assignor, who is the person entitled to the benefit of the licence or other asset, normally completes a deed of assignation in favour of the assignee, a copy of which is intimated by recorded delivery to the debtor (the person paying the licence fee), thus telling the debtor that he must henceforth pay the assignee. Without intimation to the debtor, any person who establishes a right in the asset, such as a person arresting regular licence fees in the hands of the debtor, will have priority over the assignee.

Assignation is normally done in writing, and there are suggested styles in the Transmission of Moveable Property (Scotland) Act 1862, along with methods of intimation. At the expiry of the period of assignation, as for example when an assignee's loan to an assignor is repaid (as on the occasion of a discharge of standard security for which an assignation of a life policy to a building society has been a contractual term of the loan), the asset is re-transferred, or more properly "retrocessed", to the assignor and the relevant documents returned to him.

**Security over shares**
A creditor wishing to obtain security over a debtor's shares in a company must arrange for the debtor to transfer the shares to the creditor using a stock transfer form and intimate the transfer to the company. The creditor will issue a back letter undertaking to re-transfer the shares to the debtor on the expiry of the underlying obligation for which the security was granted. The back letter will also indicate what is to be done about matters such as voting rights, rights issues and dividend payments during the period of the creditor's ownership of the shares. If the debtor defaults on his obligation,

the creditor can sell the shares. A deposit of share certificates with a creditor, while undoubtedly inconveniencing a debtor, does not form an effective security in Scotland, although it does create an equitable mortgage in England.

### The defeat of the security holder
Although the whole point of being a secured creditor is to place the creditor in a better position than other creditors in the event of the debtor's insolvency, there are occasions under bankruptcy law when this does not take place. If a debtor attempts to place a creditor in a better position than he would otherwise have been, by means of a security, whether that security be a standard security, assignment or any other form of security, that security may be reduced by (amongst others) a creditor or the trustee in sequestration, if it is established that the security was in fact either a gratuitous alienation in terms of the Bankruptcy (Scotland) Act 1985, s. 34 or the common law, an unfair preference under the Bankruptcy (Scotland) Act 1985, s. 36, a fraudulent preference under the common law, or part of an extortionate credit transaction under the Bankruptcy (Scotland) Act 1985, s. 61. There are similar provisions under the Insolvency Act 1986, enabling liquidators to reduce the above transactions for limited companies. Liquidators may be able to set aside certain floating charges under the Insolvency Act 1986, s. 245.

## COMPANIES

Companies are no different from other debtors in that they may, from time to time, wish to borrow money and need to grant security for their borrowings. What distinguishes a company from other legal personae in this respect is that companies have to register with the Registrar of Companies most of the charges that they grant. Under the Companies Act 1985, s. 410, the undernoted types of security (more commonly known as "charges" in the context of companies) must be registered within 21 days of their creation:

(a) charges over land or interests in land (effectively standard securities);
(b) security over the uncalled capital of a company (very rare in practice nowadays);
(c) security over the following types of incorporeal moveable property, being:
    (i) book debts of the company;
    (ii) calls made but not paid for;
    (iii) goodwill;
    (iv) a patent or a licence under a patent;
    (v) a trademark;
    (vi) a copyright or a licence under a copyright;
(d) a security over a ship or aircraft or any share in a ship; and
(e) a floating charge (to be discussed later).

The period of 21 days runs from the date of creation of the charge, which is the date of execution of the charge by the company, but in the case of a standard security is 21 days from the date of registration of the standard security in the Register of Sasines or the Land Register (on which occasion the security only holder gets a real right in the heritage). Failure to register the charge within 21 days requires a petition to court for late registration (Companies Act 1985, s. 420). The danger of failing to register the charge in time is that after the 21-day period of grace, a creditor, liquidator or administrator will be able to defeat the rights of the apparently secured creditor, who will find that instead of being a secured creditor with a prior right to the company's assets over which the security has been granted, he has no such rights and is treated as an unsecured creditor. As proof of the registration of a charge, the Registrar of Companies issues a certificate of registration of charge.

Companies must also keep their own register of charges in addition to the list of charges registered at the Registrar of Companies.

Ideally companies should also register memoranda of satisfaction which are the formal notifications of discharges of charges (Companies Act 1985, s. 419).

## FLOATING CHARGES

Floating charges derive from English law and form a security which is said to float or hover over the assets of a company, present and future, however constituted. They are extremely useful for companies because with a floating charge there is no requirement to deliver the asset to the creditor — which has the virtue that the company can continue to use the assets which form part of the security. The floating charge is based on the expectation (usually enforced in the contractual arrangements between the company and its floating charge holder) that the company will always have enough by way of assets to repay the obligations due to the floating charge holder.

### Receivership

Providing the company performs its obligations to the floating charge holder, the floating charge will continue to float peacefully over the company until the debt is repaid and the floating charge discharged. Should, however, the company fail to adhere to the terms of the contractual agreements between the company and the floating charge holder, and more particularly:

(a) fail to repay the whole sum secured by the charge within a period of 21 days of being asked to do so (Insolvency Act 1986, s. 52(1)(a));

(b) have two months' interest in arrears (Insolvency Act 1986, s. 52(1)(b));

(c) be wound up either compulsorily or voluntarily (Insolvency Act 1986, s. 52(1)(c)); or should

(d) any other floating charge holder appoint a receiver (Insolvency Act 1986, s. 52(1)(d)), the floating charge holder may appoint a receiver, this process being known as "attachment" or more commonly as "crystallisation of the floating charge". In effect what happens is that the charge which had hitherto floated above the company descends upon the company and is then treated as a fixed charge. This means that no other creditors (unless they have a prior right to the relevant assets) may seize those assets instead. The receiver then has various options by way of recouping the loss due to the floating charge holder: he may keep the company trading until the debt is repaid; or he may sell the company or parts of it. The receiver's primary interest is to satisfy the floating charge holder's, and while he must be mindful of other interests such as other creditors, he is ultimately working for the benefit of the floating charge holder. In so doing he will ingather certain funds, and out of these he must take account of certain creditors with rights in priority to the following charge holders rights (Insolvency Act 1986, s. 60). This may be done either by letting them exercise their rights themselves or he may pay them out of the sums he ingathers. These creditors are creditors with a prior fixed charge of the assets in receivership, creditors who have effectually exercised diligence over the company's assets (usually by means of poinding or arrestment), the receiver's own creditors in the course of the receivership, the receiver's own fees and expenses, and finally the preferential creditors referred to in the Insolvency Act 1986, Sched. 6., these being, amongst other things, certain taxes and payments to employees.

It is important to note that a receiver may not seize assets that belong to a third party, as with goods that are being used by the company but are on hire purchase or subject to a retention of title clause.

### The anomalous position of a floating charge over heritage

It is not necessary to register a floating charge in the Register of Sasines or the Land Register, yet if the company has heritage, the floating charge on crystallisation acts as if it were changed into a standard security, to the extent of any part of the heritage that is not already subject to a prior-ranking security. However, following the controversial case of *Sharp v. Thomson* (1997), where a purchaser of a house had paid the purchase price for that house to a company that later went into receivership, and where the purchaser had not at the time of the receivership actually had the disposition in his favour recorded in the appropriate land register, the purchaser was able to keep his house and defeat the receiver. The House of Lords decision on this matter, which overturned the conventional view of a receiver's powers, was widely seen as a consumer friendly decision though a somewhat tendentious one as regards conveyancing practice.

### Ranking of floating charges

Floating charges rank in date order of priority unless there is a ranking agreement to the contrary (Companies Act 1985, s. 464(1)). Floating charges will automatically be postponed to prior-ranking fixed charges (of which standard securities in practice are by far the most common) unless again there is a ranking agreement to the contrary. In Scotland it is possible to insert a clause known as a "negative pledge" clause in a floating charge which prevents the company attempting to create any security ranking in priority to the existing floating charge. In *AIB Finance Ltd v. Bank of Scotland* (1993), inadvertently a floating charge with such a provision was registered in priority to a standard security. When the company went into receivership later, the standard security holder found that contrary to expectation its standard security did not take its normal precedence over the receiver.

**The defeat of the receiver**
A receiver may not be able to exercise his rights under a floating charge if:

(a) the floating charge was not properly registered (Insolvency Act 1986, s. 410);

(b) the floating charge was created within six months of insolvent liquidation and might therefore be an unfair preference under the Insolvency Act 1986, s. 243(1), unless it can be clearly established under s. 243(2) that the transaction for which the floating charge was created was clearly for value and without any collusive intent;

(c) the floating charge was granted within 12 months of the winding up of the company (or two years if the floating charge holder was a connected person) and the company was insolvent (subject to certain exceptions relating to any benefits given to the company after the creation of the floating charge) under the Insolvency Act 1986, s. 245;

(d) the floating charge might have been granted at any time between the presentation of a petition for an administration order of the company and the granting of that order (Insolvency Act 1986, s. 245(3)(c)) or after an administrator has already been appointed (Insolvency Act 1986, s. 11(3)(b), (c));

(e) the floating charge might be part of an extortionate credit transaction under the Insolvency Act 1986, s. 244.

**Further reading**
Forte (ed.), *Scottish Commercial Law* (Butterworths, 1997), Chap. 6.
Gloag and Henderson, *The Law of Scotland* (10th ed., W.Green, 1995).
Greene and Fletcher, *The Law and Practice of Receivership in Scotland* (2nd ed., Butterworths, 1992).
Grier, *U.K. Company Law* (Wiley, 1998), Chaps 17 and 20.
Wilson, *The Scottish Law of Debt* (2nd ed., W.Green, 1991), Chaps 7–9.

# 11. BANKRUPTCY

**The concept of bankruptcy**
Bankruptcy is a legal mechanism for allowing insolvent persons to put a limit on their indebtedness so that they can start afresh in business while giving some redress to creditors.

**The meaning of "bankruptcy"**
A bankrupt, in ordinary speech, is a person who is insolvent and cannot pay his creditors. A bankrupt may not practise certain professions, such as

a solicitor or accountant, and the terms of many employment contracts state that bankruptcy is grounds for dismissal, particularly if the employee is dealing with commercially sensitive matters. A bankrupt may not be a company director or hold certain public offices such as member of parliament.

In Scottish legal parlance, the bankrupt is commonly referred to as the *debtor*. The law on bankruptcy is regulated by the Bankruptcy (Scotland) Act 1985 ("BSA") and the old common law. The process of making a debtor bankrupt and having his affairs dealt with by an insolvency practitioner or other official is known as *sequestration*. The person who looks after the affairs of the debtor is known as the *trustee in sequestration*. There are other methods of dealing with a debtor's estate which do not involve sequestration: these include such processes as protected trust deeds and compositions and will be dealt with in due course. Together all the various methods of dealing with an insolvent debtor are known collectively as bankruptcy.

Bankruptcy applies to all legal personae (*i.e.* human beings, partnerships, limited partnerships, trusts, associations and clubs, and certain corporate bodies) (BSA, s. 6) but not to registered companies. The equivalent of bankruptcy for registered companies is liquidation.

Bankruptcy is a large and complex subject, and this text does not pretend to do more than give an overview of the major issues and procedures. In particular it does not deal with the insolvent estates of deceased persons. Those who wish to study further are advised to read McBryde, *Bankruptcy*, or Adie, *Bankruptcy.*

**Types of insolvency**
There are three main types of insolvency in Scotland. They are as follows:

(1) *Absolute insolvency*  This is where a debtor's assets are less than his liabilities, even though he is able to pay his bills as they fall due.

(2) *Practical insolvency*  This is where a debtor cannot pay his debts as they fall due, even though he may be solvent overall. Such a situation is colloquially known as a "having a cash-flow problem".

(3) *Apparent insolvency*  This is defined by the Bankruptcy (Scotland) Act 1985, s. 7 as follows:

    (a)  the debtor's sequestration in Scotland or bankruptcy in England, Wales or Northern Ireland (BSA, s. 7(1)(a));

    (b)  written notice by the debtor to his creditors that he cannot pay his debts in the ordinary course of business (BSA, s. 7(1)(b));

    (c)  the granting of a trust deed for creditors (see the end of this chapter) (BSA, s. 7(1)(c)(i));

    (d)  the expiry of the *induciae* (*i.e.* time for payment) of a charge arising out of a court decree, a registered bond or a protested bill of exchange (BSA, s. 7(1)(c)(ii);

(e) the poinding or seizure of the debtor's assets following a summary warrant for rates or taxes requiring payment of the same within 14 days (BSA, s. 7(1)(c)(iii);

(f) the adjudication of the debtor's estate (BSA, s. 7(1)(c)(iv));

(g) the sale of the debtor's assets under a landlord's sequestration for rent (BSA, s. 7(1)(c)(v));

(h) the making of a receiving order against the debtor in England or Wales (BSA, s. 7(1)(c)(vi));

(i) failure to pay a debt or debts or provide security amounting to more than £1,500 within a period of three weeks following a valid demand for that sum (BSA, s. 7(1)(d)).

Apparent insolvency ceases when the debt is repaid or when the debtor obtains his discharge.

SEQUESTRATION

Sequestration is the formal process whereby the debtor's estate is put into the hands of a trustee who will then manage or dispose of the debtor's assets in accordance with the rules of bankruptcy. The proceeds therefrom are then distributed among the debtor's creditors. The overall process is supervised and monitored by the Accountant in Bankruptcy.

**The Accountant in Bankruptcy**
The Accountant in Bankruptcy is an official whose task is to oversee the practice of bankruptcy and sequestration in Scotland. He supervises the insolvency practitioners who act as trustees in sequestration or otherwise carry out bankruptcy work, and he himself may be appointed interim trustee or permanent trustee in any sequestration. If either debtors or their trustees commit any criminal acts he may report them to the Lord Advocate for further proceedings.

**The outline of sequestration**
The outline of sequestration is as follows:

(1) a qualified applicant petitions for the debtor's sequestration;
(2) the court makes an award of sequestration of the debtor's estate;
(3) as part of the award, an interim trustee is appointed;
(4) the interim trustee convenes a first statutory meeting of creditors, on which occasion the permanent trustee is appointed; commissioners may also be appointed to assist him;

(5) the permanent trustee is vested in the debtor's estate, ingathers all the debtor's assets, investigates any relevant antecedent transactions and equalises any diligence;

(6) he then distributes the assets or the proceeds thereof amongst the creditors, taking account of secured and preferential creditors before unsecured creditors;

(7) once the estate is evacuated, the sequestration is terminated, the debtor discharged and the trustee discharged;

(8) as an alternative to the above, it is possible to use the Sched. 2 procedure which is a foreshortened version of the above, sometimes known as a small assets case; or

(9) the Sched. 2A summary administration procedure, which is similar to the Sched. 2 procedure but falls within certain low financial thresholds.

**Who may petition for sequestration?**
Under BSA, s. 5, the following may petition for sequestration:

(a) the debtor with the concurrence of a qualified creditor or creditors (BSA, s. 5(2A)) and providing that:

   (i) the total amount of the debtor's debts is not less than £1,500 (BSA, s. 5(2B)(a));
   (ii) there has been no previous award of sequestration within the period of the last five years ending on the date before the date of presentation of the petition for sequestration (BSA, s. 5(2B)(b)); and
   (iii) the debtor is either apparently insolvent or has granted a trust deed which was unable to be converted into a protected trust deed because of the valid objections of a creditor (BSA, s. 5(2B)(c));

(b) a qualified creditor or creditors provided the debtor is apparently insolvent (BSA, s. 5(2)(b)) and providing that the terms of (a) (i), (ii) and (iii) above also apply;

(c) a trustee under a trust deed (BSA, s. 5(2)(c) but only if the debtor has failed without good reason to comply with any term of the trust deed or reasonable instruction to the debtor by the trustee in connection with the trust deed, or when the trustee avers in his petition that it would be in the best interests of the creditors that an award of sequestration be made (BSA, s. 5(2C)(a) and (b)).

A qualified creditor is one who is due the sum of £1,500. Several creditors may join up so that collectively their combined debt amounts to £1,500 or more: they then may collectively sequestrate the debtor (BSA, s. 5(2)(b)). For ease of reference both a qualified creditor and a group of creditors who collectively qualify will be known hereafter as a "qualifying creditor".

**The timing of the presentation of the petition**
The debtor or a trustee acting under a trust deed may petition for a debtor's sequestration at any time (BSA, s. 8(1)(a)), and a qualifying creditor may

do the same but only where the apparent insolvency on which the qualifying creditor relies was constituted within the preceding four months (BSA, s. 8(1)(b)).

### Jurisdiction and judicial procedure

Although the Court of Session may hear a petition for sequestration, it is cheaper and more common for the petition to be heard in the sheriff court. The petition is presented to the sheriff in chambers and a "first order" is granted. A copy of the petition is sent to the Accountant in Bankruptcy (BSA, s. 5(6)). Where a debtor presents his own petition the first order will be an award of sequestration (BSA, s. 12(1)), and the date of sequestration for him will then be the date of the award (BSA, s. 12(4)). Where a creditor or a trustee under a trust deed presents the petition, the first order will be a warrant of citation under the BSA, s. 12(2) requiring the debtor to appear before the court to explain why he should not be sequestrated. In this case the date of sequestration will be the date of the warrant of citation (BSA, s. 12(4)(b)). The importance of the date of sequestration is that this is the date from which the debtor's period of sequestration runs, and it may also affect the viability of antecedent transactions.

If the debtor appears in court to present a defence or to explain that the debt for which an award of sequestration was sought has been paid, the court may entertain his defence. If instead the debtor fails to respond to the citation and does not appear, or if the creditor's or trustee's grounds for the petition are justified, the court will make the award of sequestration forthwith (BSA, s. 12(3)).

Assuming the award is granted, the sheriff clerk intimates the award to the Register of Inhibitions and Adjudications (BSA, s. 14). This means that as from the date of sequestration the debtor is prohibited from selling his heritable assets. The interim trustee, who will be appointed as part of the award (BSA, s. 13(1)), will intimate his appointment in the *Edinburgh Gazette* and will ask creditors to send in their claims to him (BSA, s. 15(6)). The interim trustee has the task of safeguarding the debtor's estate for the benefit of the creditors as a whole (BSA, s. 2(1)). The interim trustee will either be nominated by the debtor or the creditor, or the Accountant in Bankruptcy may be appointed.

### Recall of sequestration

It is possible for the debtor, a creditor, the interim trustee, the permanent trustee or the Accountant in Bankruptcy to petition for recall of an award of sequestration provided the petition for the recall is done within 10 weeks of the date of sequestration (BSA, s. 16(4)), or at any time: (a) where the debtor has either repaid in full all his debts or given adequate security for them (BSA, s. 17(1)(a)); (b) where a majority of the creditors dwell outside Scotland and it would be more convenient to have the debtor's estate dealt with elsewhere (BSA s. 17(1)(b)); (c) where there are other awards of sequestration or bankruptcy proceeding elsewhere (BSA s. 17(1)(c)).

Recall is only available through the Court of Session and if permitted the previous award of sequestration is recalled (BSA, s. 17(8)). When an award of sequestration is recalled, it is treated as if it had never taken place, whereas an appeal against an award of sequestration is an appeal on legal grounds against the decision of the courts to make such an award.

## The preservation of the debtor's estate
The interim trustee is appointed to safeguard the debtor's estate. The debtor must hand over to him all papers, assets and perishable goods (BSA, s. 18), and requires him within seven days to prepare a list of his assets and liabilities (BSA, s. 19). Using the list, the interim trustee will then prepare a preliminary statement of the debtor's affairs which should indicate whether there is likely to be any payment of a dividend to the debtor's creditors (BSA, s. 20(1)). The list and the statement are sent to the creditors four days before the first meeting of creditors (BSA, s. 20(2)), and if the debtor or his spouse is not forthcoming about his personal finances, the trustee may procure that the debtor or his spouse be required to appear before the sheriff to answer such questions as may be necessary (BSA, s. 20(4)). Once the debtor's estate is being managed by the trustee, the trustee may make the debtor complete any transaction (BSA, s. 18(2)(e)) or close down his business (BSA, s. 18(2)(g)). Equally the interim trustee may apply to the court for permission to keep the debtor's business going in order to make it more marketable later (BSA, s. 18(3)(a)(i)).

## The first statutory meeting of creditors
The interim trustee must convene a meeting of the creditors within 28 days of the date of sequestration (BSA, s. 21), but if the Accountant in Bankruptcy is the interim trustee the period may be extended to 60 days (BSA, s. 21A(1)). There must be seven days' notice of the meeting to every known creditor and the creditors must submit their vouched claims to the interim trustee at or before the meeting in order to be able to vote (BSA, s. 22(1)). The interim trustee is chairman of the meeting (BSA, s. 23(1)) but must thereupon invite the creditors to elect one of their members chairman in his stead (BSA, s. 23(1)(b)) unless no one is willing to act as chairman, in which case he remains chairman. If in the interim trustee's opinion, as stated in the preliminary statement, there are insufficient funds for a dividend to be paid, he must tell the creditors, who may query his opinion under BSA, s. 23(3)(b). If the trustee believes that in view of the small size of the debtor's assets the sequestration should proceed by the Schedule 2 procedure, the interim trustee will intimate as much to the sheriff (BSA, s. 23(4)) and the Schedule 2 procedure will then take place. There is no appeal mechanism against the trustee's decision on this matter. A distinctive feature of the Schedule 2 process is that the permanent trustee is not elected, and consequently the Accountant in Bankruptcy, rather than the creditors or commissioners, monitors the trustee's actions.

If the estate falls within the parameters for summary administration (*i.e.* the debtor's assets excluding heritage amount to less than £2,000 and his liabilities excluding sums due under heritable securities amount to less than £20,000), the interim trustee or Accountant in Bankruptcy may apply to the sheriff for a grant of a certificate of summary administration (BSA, s. 23A(1)–(3)). This enables the trustee to carry out such work as will benefit the estate but does not require him to take every possible step to ingather the debtor's assets where it would be cost ineffective to do so. In this case Schedule 2A applies to the duties of the permanent trustee who, as with Schedule 2, is also unelected.

Assuming the debtor's estate is sufficiently large not to warrant the Schedule 2 or Schedule 2A procedure, the creditors will elect a permanent trustee (BSA, s. 24(1)) who may be the interim trustee. If there are no creditors present, the interim trustee will inform the sheriff, who will appoint the interim trustee to be the permanent trustee (BSA, s. 24(4)) and the Schedule 2 procedure will follow forthwith (BSA, s. 24(5)). If the Accountant in Bankruptcy already is the interim trustee, and no meeting is called, or if a meeting is called but no voting creditor attends, or if no permanent trustee is elected, the Accountant in Bankruptcy or his nominee is appointed the permanent trustee (BSA, s. 23(3A) and s. 25A(1),(2)) and the Schedule 2 or as appropriate the Schedule 2A procedure may follow thereon. The permanent trustee must be an insolvency practitioner (BSA, s. 24(2)).

At the first statutory meeting the creditors may elect committee members, known as commissioners, to advise the trustee (BSA, s. 30). He is not always obliged to follow their advice and they receive no remuneration or expenses (BSA, s. 4). Their role is to supervise the process of realisation of the debtor's estate and to inspect the trustee's intromissions.

### The permanent trustee

Assuming there are no objections to the appointment of the permanent trustee, the sheriff on receiving the interim trustee's report on the statutory meeting will confirm the permanent trustee's appointment and issue an "act and warrant" to the permanent trustee (BSA, s. 25(2)). The interim trustee is discharged (BSA, s. 27).

The permanent trustee is said to be "vested" in the debtor's estate, backdated to the date of sequestration (BSA, s. 31(8)). This means that the debtor no longer has any title to the assets in the estate, and equally that the permanent trustee can sign documents such as dispositions and validly transfer title (BSA, s. 31). The interim trustee has no such power except in the case of perishable goods (BSA, s. 18(2)(c)).

The permanent trustee has considerable powers to dispose of the debtor's estate. His duties are set out in the BSA, s. 3, one of them being reporting to the Accountant in Bankruptcy any actions by the debtor which may be criminal in nature (BSA, s. 3(3)).

Not all assets of the debtor are vested in the permanent trustee: the trustee has limited rights over *acquirenda* (as discussed later) or over property which is required for the upkeep and aliment of his family (BSA, s. 33(1)(a)). Assets held by the debtor in trust for another do not vest in the trustee (BSA, s. 33(1)(b)) and goods subject to a landlord's hypothec for rent as followed up by a sequestration for rent cannot be taken by the trustee (BSA, s. 33(2)).

### The position of *acquirenda*

*Acquirenda* is income (usually earnings) that the debtor acquires after the date of sequestration, and is deemed to belong to the debtor (BSA, s. 32(1)). However, the sheriff may, if necessary, order that a certain amount be deducted from the debtor's earnings to aliment his family and himself (BSA, s. 32(2)) and the balance applied to the permanent trustee (see *Brown's Trustee v. Brown* (1994)).

Income that a debtor receives after sequestration cannot be touched by diligence arising out of debt due at the date of sequestration (BSA, s. 32(5)).

As regards capital coming into the hands of the debtor, if it does so in the period of sequestration, the trustee is entitled to obtain it (BSA, s. 32(6)) (see *Alliance and Leicester Building Society v. Murray's Trustee* (1995)).

Where the debtor has any change in his financial circumstances, such as receiving a large bequest, he is obliged to tell the trustee of these facts and failure to do so is a criminal offence (BSA, s. 32(7).

## SWELLING THE DEBTOR'S ESTATE

A major task of the permanent trustee, a trustee under a trust deed or a judicial factor is to maximise the extent of the debtor's estate by examining transactions carried out by the debtor in the period leading up to the sequestration or, as the case may be, the apparent insolvency of the debtor. Such transactions are often known as antecedent transactions. Antecedent transactions may be reduced by the above persons (BSA, s. 34(1)(b)), or by a creditor due money in respect of a debt incurred on or before the date of sequestration, or before the granting of a trust deed by the debtor or the debtor's death as the case may be (BSA, s. 34(1)(b)). For the purposes of this chapter and to avoid repetition any of the above individuals who are entitled to challenge an antecedent transaction will be known as a "challenger". Following a successful challenge, the recipient of an antecedent transaction will be required, under certain circumstances, to return the assets or their value, and the assets or their cash equivalent will then be added to the pool of assets distributable to the creditors generally.

Certain of the following antecedent transactions may be challenged both under statute or under common law.

The challengeable antecedent transactions are as follows:

(a) gratuitous alienations (BSA, s. 34);

(b) the recalling of a capital sum on divorce (BSA, s. 35);

(c) unfair preferences (BSA, s. 36) and fraudulent preferences;

(d) excessive pension contributions (BSA, ss. 36A–36C);

(e) diligence carried out within certain periods relative to the date of sequestration or the onset of apparent insolvency (BSA, s. 37 and Sched. 7, para. 24);

(f) extortionate credit transactions (BSA, s. 61).

### Reduction of gratuitous alienations under statute

A gratuitous alienation is the term for a gift, the transfer of an asset for less than full value or the renunciation of a claim or a right (BSA, s. 34(2)(a)) . It is challengeable by any of the challengers (BSA, s. 34(1)) where any of (a), (b) or (c) have taken place, together with (d):

(a) the sequestration of the debtor's estate (BSA, s. 34(2)(b)(i));

(b) the granting of a trust deed which subsequently is protected (BSA, s. 34(2)(b)(ii));

(c) the death of the debtor and the sequestration of his estate within 12 months of his death (BSA, s. 34(2)(b)(iii));

(d) the alienation took place on a relevant day (BSA, s. 34(2)(c)).

A relevant day is the day that the alienation became completely effectual (for example, a standard security is only effectual on registration in the Register of Sasines, not on execution), but it also depends on who the recipient is. If the recipient is an *associate* of the debtor, the relevant day is any date within a period of five years prior to the date of sequestration, the granting of the trust deed or the death of the debtor (BSA, s. 34(3)(a)). An associate is defined in the BSA, s. 74 as effectively a close relative, an employer or employee, a partner or a company of which the debtor is a director. If the recipient is not an associate, the period is of two years' duration only.

There are exemptions to the above rule. If the person seeking to maintain the validity of the alienation can establish any of the following, the alienation will not be reduced:

(a) at the time of the alienation or at any other time after the alienation the debtor's assets were greater than his liabilities (BSA, s. 34(4)(a));

(b) the alienation was made for adequate consideration (BSA, s. 34(4)(b));

(c) the alienation was a birthday, Christmas or some other conventional gift (such as a wedding present), or was made for a charitable purpose to someone who was not an associate of the debtor, and it was reasonable to have made the alienation (BSA, s. 34(4)(c)).

Where a recipient has sold a gratuitously alienated asset to a third party who acquired it in good faith and for value, the third party is not required to deliver the asset back to the trustee. The recipient instead would have to pay the value of the alienated asset back to the sequestrated estate. This is permitted by the wording of the BSA, s. 43(4) which allows the court to grant reduction " for such restoration of property to the debtor's estate or other redress as may be appropriate". It would appear from the case *Short's Trustee v. Chung* (1991) that reduction is the preferred remedy and only where that is impossible or inappropriate will some other form of redress be allowed.

If a recipient of a gratuitous alienation receives an asset from the debtor for less than adequate consideration, he still has to return the asset to the debtor's estate, even though he may have paid some money for it, and he may claim against the estate as a creditor in respect of what he did pay — but only as a postponed creditor (BSA, s. 51(3)(c)).

The term "adequate consideration" was considered in *McFadyen's Trustee v. McFadyen* (1994), where it was held that consideration is to be given its normal meaning and has to mean that something of material or patrimonial value is paid.

A further exemption arises under the BSA, s. 34(7), whereby life assurance policies written under the protection of the Married Women's Policies of Assurance (Scotland) Act 1880 in favour of one's spouse and children are protected from reduction.

### Reduction of gratuitous alienations under the common law

Under common law once a person becomes insolvent he holds his assets as trustee for creditors, and any alienation that is for less than full value may be reduced by a challenger unless it can be proved that it was in fulfilment of some proper obligation contracted during solvency. Whereas under statute it is for the person founding on the gratuitous alienation to defend its validity, under the common law the challenger has: (a) to prove that the alienation was gratuitous or for less than full value; and (b) that the debtor was absolutely insolvent, either at the time of the alienation, or as a result of the alienation, and has remained absolutely insolvent since the alienation — which might in practice, unless the challenger had access to the debtor's accounts, be difficult to establish. Under the common law the statutory time limits do not apply, and a challenge does not need to wait until sequestration or some other event. As a result of these practical problems, the common law is not in practice much used. It was used in *Boyle's Trustee v. Boyle* (1988), where the debtor was paying money to his wife for her to have a home to live in. The trustee successfully challenged the payments on the grounds that such payments did not form an obligation properly contracted for while the debtor was still solvent.

### Recalling a capital sum paid on divorce

If a debtor pays a capital sum to his spouse as part of their divorce settlement, and if at the time he was either absolutely insolvent or became so as a result of the payment, and within five years he: (a) is sequestrated; (b) grants a trust deed which becomes protected; (c) dies and within 12 months his estate is sequestrated; or (d) dies and within 12 months a judicial factor is appointed over his estate, the court may make an order recalling the order for the repayment of the capital sum to the estate (BSA, s. 35). This may be made by any of the challengers referred to earlier with the exception of creditors.

### Unfair preferences (under statute)

Unfair preferences arise when a debtor wishes to place certain creditors in a better position than other creditors, usually because he hopes to retain the creditors' continued goodwill after his bankruptcy. It is sometimes done by giving a creditor a security for an unsecured debt or by repaying a favoured creditor long before payment is due. Under the BSA, s. 36(1), an unfair preference may be challenged by any of the challengers as in gratuitous alienations (BSA, s. 36(4) if the preference was created not more than six months before: (a) the date of sequestration of the debtor's estate; or (b) the granting of a trust deed which becomes protected.

Under the BSA, s. 36(2), there are certain transactions which are exempt from challenge, these being:

(a) a transaction in the ordinary course of business;

(b) a payment in cash for a debt that was due to be paid, unless the transaction for which the cash was paid was collusive with the purpose of depriving other creditors of funds;

(c) a transaction in which each party undertook reciprocal obligations, either simultaneously or over a period of time, unless as in (b) it was collusive;

(d) the granting of a mandate by a debtor authorising an arrestee to pay over arrested funds to the arresting creditor.

Assuming the challenge is successful the court will reduce the transaction and the subject of the transaction will be returned to the estate (see *Balcraig House's Trustee v. Roosevelt Property Services* (1994)) unless some other redress may be more appropriate (BSA, s. 36(5)), always providing that the rights of third parties acquiring assets, originally the subject of an unfair preference, in good faith and for value, are protected (BSA, s. 36(5)).

It would appear that collusion (see (b) above) requires the involvement of both parties to the collusion. In *Nordic Travel Ltd v. Scotprint Ltd* (1980), the creditor, knowing that the debtor was insolvent, wanted payment in cash. Although this might have appeared collusive, it was not so because the transaction in question was in the ordinary course of business and a payment in cash does not automatically imply collusion.

The reciprocal obligation exemption (sometimes known as the *nova debita* exemption) is unobjectionable because the estate is simultaneously losing an asset but receiving some other asset or benefit. Accordingly the overall estate is not deprived of anything (see *Nicoll v. Steelpress (Supplies) Ltd* (1992)).

**Fraudulent preferences under the common law**
This is the same concept as an unfair preference. The qualifications for reducing a fraudulent preference are that the preference must have been voluntary; the debtor must have been aware of his own insolvency; have must have been absolutely insolvent at the time of the preference and have remained insolvent to the date of the challenge. As a matter of practice these are usually difficult facts for a challenger to be able to establish. The potential challengers are the same as in statute (BSA, s. 36(6)). In *Wiley, Stewart and Marshall v. Jervis* (1913), an insolvent son transferred half of his house to his father who had lent him the money to buy the house. The disposition was accordingly reduced as a fraudulent preference. There are very similar exemptions to the statutory exemptions. The advantages of the common law rules are that the period of time during which the transaction may be challenged is up to five years, instead of the very short six months, and there is no need to wait for sequestration.

**Excessive pension contributions**
A debtor might well be tempted to pay large quantities of his money into a pension fund to be held in trust until his retirement. This is now struck at by BSA, ss. 36A–36C. These subsections state that the courts can reduce excessive payments into the debtor's pension fund over the five years preceding the award of sequestration and substitute reasonable payments thereto instead (BSA, s. 36B).

**Equalisation of diligence**
Diligence is the process whereby a creditor, with the benefit of court judgment or certain instruments of debt which can command summary diligence (*i.e.* where no court judgment is required for enforcement because the debtor has already consented to diligence), may instruct messengers at

arms (for the Court of Session) or sheriff officers (for the sheriff court) to enforce the creditor's rights of payment. Nowadays, the common forms of diligence are inhibition, poinding and arrestment. Inhibition is a process whereby the debtor may not transfer any heritage or grant any security over any heritage that he may own. If he tries to do so, the creditor may set aside the transaction. The inhibition is released by a discharge of inhibition, which is usually only available once the creditor has been paid. Poinding is the forcible seizure of the debtor's assets. Following a carefully controlled procedure, the debtor's goods will be itemised, valued and ultimately sold at auction and the proceeds (which are generally paltry) remitted to the creditor. Arrestment is the seizure of the debtor's assets in the hands of a third party, such as the debtor's money in a bank account or his furniture in a depositary. Once the asset is arrested, the debtor may consent to its release to the creditor by means of a mandate to the holder of the asset to do so, or the creditor may have to proceed to an action of furthcoming which compels the holder to release the assets to the creditor.

One of the virtues of sequestration is that a debtor's creditors can no longer carry out diligence against him once he is sequestrated.

Creditors who are keenest to carry out diligence on the debtor's assets are the ones likely to be repaid first at the expense of other creditors who have waited. The law of Scotland deems this to be unfair on the less aggressive creditors and treats all creditors within certain time periods as having all carried out their diligence on the same day ("the equalisation date"). All the seized assets are pooled and the trustee divides up the assets *pari passu* amongst all the creditors, though certain creditors who carried out diligence are entitled to the expenses of their diligences as a first call on the assets.

There are two forms of equalisation, one based on apparent insolvency under the BSA, s. 75(1)(b) and Sched. 7, para. 24, and one based on sequestration (BSA, s. 37).

Equalisation involving apparent insolvency may take place even though the debtor has not been sequestrated. It extends for a period of 60 days prior to the date of apparent insolvency and for a period of four months afterwards, making six months in total. In exceptional circumstances there can be repeated apparent insolvencies, which complicate the position considerably. Equalisation based on apparent insolvency has the result that all diligences on one asset within the relevant six month period are treated as ranking equally, so no one creditor gets more than his fair share out of the proceeds of sale of that asset. Equalisation based on apparent insolvency does not apply to inhibitions.

More commonly, equalisation involves sequestration and the equalisation date is the actual date of sequestration (BSA, s. 37), but the period of equalisation is only 60 days prior to sequestration. Poindings, arrestments and inhibitions within the period of equalisation are cut down (not merely ranking equally as in equalisation based on apparent insolvency) and in respect of poindings and arrestments assets have to be handed to the trustee (BSA, s. 37(4)), though the poinding and arresting creditors may obtain their expenses. Inhibitors have no assets to hand back and they lose any preferential position they may have had with regard to the debtor's heritage

(BSA, s. 37(2)). They may not obtain the expenses of the inhibition. If a debtor had granted a standard security after an inhibition, the trustee would have the benefit of the inhibitor's right to challenge the grant of the standard security (BSA, s. 37(3)).

Sequestration itself has the effect of equalising all creditors generally as at the date of sequestration (BSA, s. 37(1)).

The effect of all these rules is that within certain time limits no one creditor can obtain preferential rights to the debtor's assets at the expense of the other creditors. However, diligence fully completed *before* the onset of the 60-day period (in either case) cannot be revoked by the trustee. A pre-equalisation period inhibitor retains a prior ranking over equalisation period creditors (BSA, s. 31(2)). A landlord's hypothec is not affected by the equalisation of diligence rules (BSA, s. 33(2)). Diligence *after* the date of sequestration gives no preference to the creditor effecting diligence (BSA, s. 35(2)) and he must instead intimate his claim to the trustee.

### Extortionate credit transactions

Under the BSA, s. 61 where the terms on which a debt requires to be repaid are deemed to be extortionate, the court, on the application of the permanent trustee, may set aside the transaction in whole or in part or otherwise, at its discretion, vary the transaction. The creditor would then be required to return any excessive payments to the trustee. It is for the creditor to prove that the terms of the transaction are fair and not extortionate. The transaction in question must have been entered into within three years of the date of sequestration.

## MANAGEMENT OF THE ESTATE

The trustee will carry out as necessary the above methods of swelling the estate, but he may if he thinks it appropriate, and with the advice and consent of the commissioners, the creditors and the courts as the case may be, continue the debtor's business to raise more funds with which to pay creditors or may raise court actions (BSA, s. 39). Commonly the trustee proceeds to sell as much of the debtor's estate as he is permitted to sell. Where the debtor has heritage over which there is a standard security, either the heritable creditor or the trustee may sell the heritage, but each must account to the other so that the heritable creditor receives his debt in full and the surplus, if any, is handed to the trustee (BSA, s. 39(4)). There are also procedures under Schedule 1 to enable the trustee to have the heritable security assigned to him in return for payment of the secured debt. The trustee must have regard to the rights of the debtor's spouse and children (BSA, s. 40) and if the debtor or his family believe that the sale of the house is premature, they may apply to the court for a delay in the sale.

### Examination of the debtor

Sometimes it is necessary for the debtor to be examined in public or in private, before the trustee or before a sheriff (BSA, ss. 44–47). The advantage of a private examination is that a "quiet chat" may reveal more than a more formal examination; the advantage of a public examination is that the presence of creditors, the panoply of the law and cross-examination in the atmosphere of a court room may put pressure on the debtor to reveal what he ought to reveal.

## Creditors' claims

Creditors must supply their vouched claims (and indeed will generally already have done so if they attended the first meeting of creditors) which will, if accepted, entitle them to draw a dividend from the debtor's estate (BSA, ss. 48–50). Where the trustee rejects a claim, there are procedures available for the creditor to appeal to the sheriff (BSA, s. 49(6)). Where a creditor is both due money to a debtor and is due money from a debtor, he may exercise set-off, provided the pre-insolvency debts are kept separate from the post-insolvency debts.

## Distribution of estate

The debtor's estate, once fully ingathered, is distributed to the various creditors in the following order of priority (BSA, s. 51(1)):

(a) the outlays and remuneration of the interim trustee;
(b) the outlays and remuneration of the permanent trustee;
(c) where the debtor has died, his deathbed and funeral expenses and the expenses of administering his estate;
(d) where a creditor has petitioned for sequestration, the creditor's expenses;
(e) preferred debts ( to be discussed shortly);
(f) ordinary debts (*i.e.* unsecured creditors' debts);
(g) interest on preferred debts and on ordinary debts;
(h) any postponed debt.

A *preferred* debt is one of the debts in Part I of Schedule 3 to the BSA and covers certain debts to the Inland Revenue, debts due to Customs and Excise, social security contributions, contributions to occupational pension schemes and certain payments to employees. These creditors are sometimes known as the preferential creditors.

*Ordinary* debts include any debt due to a heritable creditor which was not satisfied by the sale of a property.

A *postponed* debt is either a loan from the debtor to his business where his business is a partnership, or a loan made to the debtor by his spouse, or the value of an asset that formed part of a gratuitous alienation which was challenged by the trustee (BSA s. 51(3)).

It is unusual for an estate to be quickly divided: some bankruptcies take some years to be sorted out and the creditors receive small payments over a period of time. Frequently there are insufficient assets for all creditors to be repaid in full and the ordinary creditors may agree to settle for a percentage of what they are due. The trustee's accounts require to be exhibited to the commissioners and the Accountant in Bankruptcy (BSA, s. 53).

If at the end of the day there is any surplus, it is returned to the debtor or his successors (BSA, s. 51(5)).

**The debtor**

After three years the debtor is automatically discharged (BSA, s. 54(1)) unless the permanent trustee or a creditor applies to the court to have the debtor's period of bankruptcy extended by up to a further two years (BSA, s. 54(4)). Once the debtor is discharged, he is free to be a company director again and to hold public office.

Until the debtor is discharged he is subject, under pain of prosecution (BSA, s. 67), to various requirements to inform the trustee of any concurrent proceedings elsewhere and to co-operate with the trustee generally.

**The discharge of the permanent trustee**

The permanent trustee may apply for his discharge once he has made his final division of the estate, and assuming the Accountant in Bankruptcy is satisfied with the trustee's accounts and all other documentation including his sederunt book (his record of all transactions and accounts), he will in due course receive his certificate of discharge (BSA, s. 57).

## ALTERNATIVE METHODS OF DEALING WITH DEBTORS' ESTATES

### Compositions

A composition is where the creditors agree to discharge a debtor in exchange for part payment of their debts. It may sometimes arise where a member of the debtor's family agrees to reinvest in the debtor so that by the refloating of his business he may ultimately repay his creditors in full. If this is done judicially it is known as a general composition. The proposed terms are offered to the Accountant in Bankruptcy and, if approved, to the creditors. A dividend of at least 25p in the pound must be payable to the creditors if the composition is to proceed. A two-thirds majority (in value) of the creditors must approve the composition and the sheriff is asked to consider and approve the composition. If approved by him the composition proceeds according to its terms (BSA, Sched. 4).

Compositions are not greatly used because any creditor who does not approve of the terms of the composition remains free to carry out diligence against the debtor, thus probably making it harder for the debtor to fulfil the term of the composition. If the debtor defaults on his undertakings in the composition, creditors may resume their actions against him.

### Schedule 2 procedure

The Bankruptcy (Scotland) Act 1993 was introduced to save money because public funds were being used at an excessive rate to pay the remuneration for trustees in sequestration. Henceforth the Accountant in Bankruptcy is to be used instead as interim or permanent trustee in small assets cases, thus saving public funds.

The Schedule 2 procedure is like a simplified version of normal sequestration. The trustee is appointed rather than elected. The Accountant or his nominee is the trustee and he has wide authority to realise the estate in the manner of a permanent trustee.

## Summary procedure

In a sequestration it may happen that the extent of the debtor's assets is so small that it is not worthwhile justifying the considerable expense of investigating every claim that the estate might make. Accordingly it is open to a trustee to apply to the court for a certificate of summary administration which permits him to reduce the amount of work to what will be of use to the estate and no more. The trustee may apply for such a certificate where the aggregate amount of the debtor's assets excluding heritage does not exceed £2,000 and the aggregate amount of his debts excluding heritable securities amounts to £20,000 (BSA, s. 23A). The duties of the trustee once appointed in terms of the certificate are outlined in Schedule 2A and are broadly similar to the ordinary duties of a permanent trustee, save that the trustee is not required to expend time and money on activities which in his view would be unprofitable for the estate as a whole.

## Trust deeds for creditors

A trust deed for creditors was originally a method whereby a debtor could convey to a trust such of his estate as could be agreed upon by all the creditors. The trust would then be administered by the trustee for the creditors. Much depends on the wording of the trust deed, the co-operation of the debtor, and the willingness of the creditors. Although a trust deed is a creature of the common law, there are certain provisions under the BSA, Sched. 5 which apply to trust deeds, namely that the debtor, creditor or the trustee himself may require that the trustee's accounts be audited by the Accountant in Bankruptcy, irrespective of any contrary provision in the trust deed. There are other provisions designed to reinforce the rights and obligations of the trustee relative to the debtor and the creditor. However, a trust deed's major failing is that any creditor who does not accede to the trust deed is not bound by it, and may continue with action against the debtor. As this may be vexatious for the other creditors, ordinary trust deeds are rarely used, though it is possible for the trust deeds to be "protected trust deeds" which more effectively safeguard the remaining creditors and the debtor from the predations of the non-acceding creditor.

## The protected trust deed

If a trust deed fulfils certain conditions specified in Schedule 5, including the requirement to transfer to a trust the debtor's entire estate with the exception of vital necessities for himself and his family, the trust deed may be protected. The conditions are that all known creditors, to whom intimation of the proposed trust deed has been made, must, to the extent of a majority in number or at least a third in value, either assent to the terms of the trust deed or fail to notify the proposed trustee (who must be an insolvency practitioner qualified to be a trustee in sequestration) of their objections within five weeks. If this is done the trust will be protected and the protected trust deed registered with the Accountant in Bankruptcy. Those creditors who have done nothing are deemed to have accepted the deed. A validly objecting creditor has a period of six weeks from the date of the original intimation to apply to the court for sequestration, and the creditor may also apply at any time for the debtor's sequestration if he can prove to the court that the distribution by the trustee is unfairly prejudicial to that creditor's interests. The trustee himself may apply for the debtor's sequestration where the debtor has unreasonably not adhered to the terms of the trust deed or failed to comply with a reasonable instruction from the trustee (BSA, s. 5(2C)). The debtor may not apply for sequestration while the trust deed is in operation. The protected trust deed has proved considerably more popular than the trust deed. The trustee pays out the estate in the same manner as a trustee in sequestration and the whole process may be cheaper, easier, and less embarrassing for the debtor than sequestration. It may even result in a quicker discharge both of the debtor and ultimately of the trustee.

**Further reading**
Adie, *Bankruptcy* (Institute of Chartered Accountants in Scotland/W. Green, 1997).
Forte (ed.), *Scots Commercial Law* (Butterworths, 1997), Chap. 7.
Gloag and Henderson, *The Law of Scotland* (10th ed., W. Green, 1995), Chap. 54.
McBryde, *Bankruptcy* (2nd ed., W. Green, 1995).
McKenzie, "Gratuitous Alienations and Unfair Preferences on Insolvency" (1993) 38 J.L.S.S. 141.

---

# APPENDIX: SAMPLE EXAMINATION QUESTIONS AND ANSWERS

These questions are adapted from recent examination questions at the University of Edinburgh and Napier University, whose permission for their use is gratefully acknowledged.

1. *On December 1, 19X9, Jim informs Angus of Angus Mighty Motors Ltd, a car dealer, that he wishes to buy a tough all-weather four wheel drive vehicle for his remote farm in Argyll. Angus, who has visited the farm, informs Jim that he has a vehicle which in his opinion should be able to cope with the demanding conditions Jim experiences at his farm. The vehicle, known as the Highlander, is new on the market and on Angus's suggestion, Jim takes the vehicle for a test drive through Oban. Jim professes himself satisfied with the vehicle and pays for the vehicle before driving it home to his farm. Just before he leaves, he notices a specialised tow-truck which happens to be very well designed for Jim's other car. As he has been looking for this model of tow-truck for a long time, and as the model has recently gone out of production, he agrees to buy it and pays for it, but tells Angus that he will pick it up when he next brings his other car into Oban. Angus agrees to look after it until then. Jim then drives home, without difficulty, in his new Highlander.*

*A month later, Jim is driving the Highlander on his farm when it gets stuck in the mud and he has to be rescued. This happens again the following week, whereupon Jim reads in a car magazine that according to tests, the Highlander is an excellent vehicle for rocky tracks but is very unsatisfactory in fields where its weight and its unmanoeuvrability often results in it becoming stuck. Furthermore the windscreen wipers do not work properly. Jim writes to Angus to ask for his money back, and Angus refuses to let him have it. To add injury to insult, when Jim telephones Angus, Angus inadvertently lets slip that by mistake they had sold the tow-truck to somebody else who had taken it away and they cannot find a replacement. Advise Jim.*

This question deals with the Sale of Goods Act 1979 ("SOGA") and in particular with section 14 (implied term about quality or fitness). There are various issues arising from the question, amongst which are fitness for the purpose for which the vehicle was acquired, the opportunity given to Jim to inspect the vehicle, the sale by the seller in possession and the unsatisfactory quality of the wipers.

It is clear that Jim had made known to Angus the particular purpose for which he wished to use the vehicle, and that under SOGA, s. 14 there is an implied term of the contract between Jim and Angus that the vehicle will be reasonably fit for his particular purpose. This implied term can only be set aside where Angus can show that Jim was not relying on Angus's skill and judgment, or that it was unreasonable of Jim to rely on Angus's skill and judgment.

On the facts given in the question it would appear that Jim sought Angus's advice on vehicles to cope with tough conditions, and having done so it would appear that he was relying on Angus's skill and judgment (SOGA, s. 14 (3)). As Angus knew Jim's farm, it would not be unreasonable to rely on Angus's skill and judgment. In this respect the situation is different from that in *Griffiths v. Peter Conway Ltd* (1939), where the plaintiff failed to draw the seller's attention to the plaintiff's particular circumstances and accordingly the seller was not liable.

Angus might however claim that as Jim had had an opportunity to test the vehicle before he bought it, he was precluded from rejecting the vehicle later. It is true that Jim had such an opportunity, but he was not given the opportunity to drive it in the conditions that could exist at his farm, and it would not therefore be apparent that the vehicle might be unsuitable for those conditions (SOGA, s. 14(2C)(b)). He could therefore claim damages (SOGA, s. 15B(1)(a)) or treat the unsuitability of the car as a material breach and reject the goods (SOGA, s. 15B(1)(b)). It is arguable how material the breach is, but if he were a consumer, which by virtue of his being a farmer and acting in the course of his business he is not (see also Consumer Credit Act 1974, s. 35), he could not have the benefit of the SOGA, s. 15B(2) which would have given a clearer indication of the materiality qualification. It is arguable that Jim should have rejected the vehicle sooner. Under SOGA, s. 34 Jim is allowed a reasonable opportunity to see if the vehicle is in accordance with his contract and, in particular, for the purpose for which he bought the vehicle. It is up to Jim to ask for the reasonable opportunity and the question does not say that he did ask for this. On the other hand, a month is not a very long time so it would have to be a matter of judgment for the court to decide whether or not a month was reasonable under the circumstances (SOGA, s. 59).

If Jim does succeed in claiming damages, he may claim for the loss directly and naturally arising out of the breach by Angus in providing a vehicle that failed to perform the purpose for which it was bought (SOGA, s. 53A(1)).

Although in reality the dealer would no doubt repair the wipers free of charge, the failure of the wipers could be held to prevent the vehicle being of satisfactory quality, since under the SOGA, s. 14(2B), freedom from minor defects is one of the criteria used to establish satisfactory quality. This would in theory enable Jim to sue for damages under the SOGA, s. 15B(1), since non-working wipers could hardly be said to be a material breach of the contract. However, were Jim a consumer he would be able to reject the goods under section 15B(2) because of the wider definition of "material" in non-consumer contracts.

The inadvertent sale of the tow-truck is a sale by a seller in possession under the SOGA, s. 24. The second purchaser is entitled to keep the tow-truck and Jim is entitled to his money back.

2. *Consider the law applicable to the following situations:*

(a) *Ben steals a horse and sells it to Charles, who then sells it to David.*

(b) *Edith buys an antique chair from Frieda, paying for it with a cheque that subsequently is dishonoured by the bank. Edith then sells the chair to Gwen before Frieda tells Edith that the cheque is dishonoured and that she wants the chair back.*

(c) *Henry sends a consignment of barley to Ian for making whisky. Under the terms of their contract, Ian does not get the property in the barley until he has paid Henry. As it happens, Ian sells half the barley at a proper price to another whisky manufacturer who buys the barley unaware that Ian has not paid for it. The remaining half is still in Ian's possession when he is sequestrated.*

(d) *John undertakes to sell some specially selected frozen lamb to a restaurant which paid for it in advance. It was agreed that the risk would pass on payment. The lamb existed at the time the contract was made, but shortly after payment and before delivery to the restaurant, the electricity supply to the deep freeze unit where the lamb was stored was cut off and the meat had to be destroyed.*

(e) *Keith shows Lottie, a consumer, a sample of his new industrial cleaners. They seem to be very efficacious, so Lottie orders a considerable supply. When they are duly delivered, Lottie signs the acceptance slip stating that she has accepted and examined the goods, even though in fact she did not have time to test them there and then. She also pays the haulier who delivered the goods. It transpires later that their cleaning ability is very poor.*

(a) In this situation, Ben has no right of ownership to pass to Charles. Charles does not obtain good title and can give no better title to David than he has. When the true owner finds his horse, he is entitled to claim it back from David as it never left his ownership. David can sue Charles for breach of the implied term in the SOGA, s. 12(1) that Charles had the right to sell the goods. A suitable case in point is *Rowland v. Divell* (1923).

(b) Whereas question (a) dealt with a title that was void, (b) deals with a title that is voidable. Edith tricked Frieda into a fraudulent sale, but it remains a sale up to the point where Frieda challenges the sale. Under SOGA, s. 23, where the title has not been avoided by the time of the sale to Gwen, Gwen acquires good title to the goods, provided she buys in good faith and without notice of the defect in Edith's title to the goods. Accordingly Frieda's remedy, such as it is, is to find Edith and sue her for the value of the chair.

(c) The contract between Henry and Ian contains a retention of title clause, which in the normal course of events should ensure that while payment for the barley is still outstanding the barley remains in the ownership of Henry, even if it is in the possession of Ian. Accordingly the half of the barley that is remaining on Ian's sequestration must be returned to Henry as it never left Henry's ownership, and Ian's trustee in sequestration may not retain it. The barley that was sold to another whisky manufacturer may remain with the other manufacturer, provided he bought the barley in good faith and without any notice of any right of Henry's in the original barley (SOGA, s. 25(1)). Henry would have to lodge a claim with Ian's trustee in sequestration for the value of the barley that had been sold on.

(d) This question refers to the perishing of goods. In this case there is no fault on either the buyer's or the seller's part, unless one takes the view that there ought to have been a back-up electricity generator. Assuming there is no fault, and given that the risk was specifically said to pass on payment, the restaurant has to bear the loss (SOGA, s. 20(1)), and should have insured against the loss of the meat from the time of payment when the risk passed to the restaurant. If the power cut is attributable to the fault of John, he may be liable for the loss (SOGA, s. 20(2)) and he may also be liable to the restaurant generally under a duty of care as a custodier of the meat (SOGA, s. 20(3)).

(e) This question concerns the buyer's right to examine the goods. Keith must allow Lottie a reasonable opportunity to examine the goods to see if they conform with the sample she was shown before (SOGA, s. 34). Even though she apparently intimates that she has accepted the goods, under section 35 if she has not had the chance to examine them she is not deemed to have accepted the goods, and will not be deemed to have accepted the goods until she has carried out her examination (SOGA, s. 35(2)), even if she agreed otherwise, as the contract in question is a consumer contract (SOGA, s. 35(3)).

3. *(a) Explain how a simple unindorsed bill of exchange operates. How can it be transferred to another person?*

*(b) How does the law on bills of exchange serve to protect the holder in due course of a bill of exchange?*

*(c) In what respects does a cheque differ from a bill of exchange?*

(a) A bill of exchange is an order in writing addressed by the drawer of the bill to the drawee (the person who is to pay the bill) requiring him to pay at a fixed or determinable date (which may be on demand, on sight, on a certain date, or on so many days after a certain date) a sum certain in money (which may include interest) to the payee or to the payee's order (Bills of Exchange Act 1882 ("BOE"), s. 3). The payee may be the drawer.

Normally the drawer tells the drawee of the bill, and the drawee will accept the bill on a preliminary basis to acknowledge that he will have to pay the bill at the due date (at which stage the drawee becomes known as the acceptor). If the bill is a demand bill, acceptance does not arise and the bill should be paid on demand. Assuming that the bill is payable at a later date, the accepted bill is delivered to the payee. On the date for payment the bill will be presented for payment and payment will be made. This discharges the bill.

If the bill is not accepted, the payee may ultimately claim against the drawer for issuing him with a bill that the drawee cannot or will not accept (BOE, s. 43(2)). If the bill is accepted but not paid, the payee may again claim against the drawer (BOE, s. 47(2)). The claim is done by way of noting and protest before a notary public, which allows the payee to execute summary diligence against the drawer.

Bills may be made payable to bearer, in which case they may be transferred by delivery to someone else (BOE, s. 31(2)), or they may be payable to the order of the payee. If they are marked non-negotiable, then anyone who takes the bill from the payee does so in the knowledge that he will get no better title to the bill than the payee (BOE, s. 35). A bill made out to order means that the payee may, if he wishes, order someone else to have the benefit of the bill. He will do this by negotiating the bill to a transferee. This is done by indorsement which is signing the bill. The indorsee may in turn indorse the bill to someone else.

(b) A holder in due course is a person who has had a bill transferred to him. Provided he acquires the bill in good faith for a proper price, without notice of any defect in the transferor's title, and provided the bill is valid on the face of it and not overdue, he will be entitled to receive payment from the drawee, whom failing the drawer or any previous indorsee of the bill (BOE, s. 29(1)). This places the holder in due course in a better position sometimes than the person who transferred the bill of exchange to him, and may mean that a person who has wrongfully obtained a bill of exchange may give a better title than he himself had. This rule does not apply where there has been forgery of any party's signature (BOE, s. 24), though a drawee is not allowed to claim that a drawer's signature is forged by way of an attempt to avoid paying the bill (BOE, s. 54(2)).

(c) A cheque differs little in principle from a bill of exchange, save that a cheque is always payable on demand and always drawn on a banker (BOE, s. 73). Cheques are regulated by the BOE and by the Cheques Acts 1957 and 1992. Banks are given special protection under statute so that if they inadvertently, but in good faith and in the ordinary course of business, pay out an uncrossed cheque to a person who has stolen that cheque, they will not be held liable to their customer for paying the thief, since they become in their own right holders in due course. Nowadays nearly all cheques are crossed which means that they may only be paid into a bank account. This means that a thief stealing a cheque would have to set up a bank account into which the cheque could be paid, though if a bank was unwise enough to pay out cash on a crossed cheque, it would have to reimburse both its customer and the true owner of the cheque. Cheques may be indorsed in favour of another person, though a cheque that is marked "non-negotiable" means that the transferee can get no better title than the transferor.

Cheques go stale after six months whereupon they need to be re-issued.

4. *Charles wishes to insure his domestic property and approaches his insurance broker to help him obtain the best quotations. He also wants to take out some life assurance and wants any proceeds of the life assurance policy to be paid to his wife if he dies within the term of the policy. Charles notices that in the domestic insurance proposal form he is required to warrant that his house is wind and watertight at the time of the commencement of the policy, and that he will take all steps to keep it so. He also notices that it is a material condition of the life assurance proposal that he is in good health. He tells his agent that he is suffering from high blood pressure and that his doctor has warned him that he must take life easy. The agent ignores this fact and writes down that Charles is in good health. Charles sees this but signs it anyway. Two weeks after the policy has commenced, Charles drops dead of a heart attack.*
   *Explain what the law is in relation to the above matters.*

A broker is a person who acts as a middleman between the insurance company and the insured. He is normally paid by commission from the insurance company. The law is unclear as to whether the broker can be treated in law as the insurer's agent or the insured's agent, but where there is a tied agency the supposition is that the broker will be the insurer's agent.

It is perfectly possible for the life assurance policy to be written in trust for his wife (Married Women's Policies of Assurance (Scotland) Act 1880).

A warranty is a statement which need not be material but which must be strictly complied with, as in *Dawson v. Bonnin*. However, to undertake to take all steps to keep the house wind and watertight is not easy and one would normally expect the proposer to be able to qualify that warranty by undertaking to take all "reasonable" steps to keep the building wind and watertight.

As regards Charles's health, even though the broker completed the proposal inaccurately Charles should have corrected it since he is under a requirement to act in the utmost good faith (*uberrimae fidei*) in the completion of the form, as in *The Spathari*. Accordingly his false declaration invalidates the policy.

5. (a) *Eve, a director of a wine bottling company, is buying a country cottage in the Highlands. She cannot afford to pay for it all herself, so she*

*takes out a loan from the bank. The bank requires her to grant a standard security over the cottage in favour of the bank. Explain to Eve what this means and what the bank's rights are in respect of this standard security.*

(b)     *Eve's company owns a large quantity of wine in large sealed vats. The wine is stored in warehouses in Leith until the time comes to bottle the wine. The wine in the vats is valuable and as the company is needing funds for expansion of its operations, Eve and her fellow directors wonder if it is possible for the company to raise a loan on the strength of the value of wine at present in the warehouses.*

*The bank agrees to lend on the strength of the value of the wine in the vats, but is unsure how to take security over the wine. How could this be done ?*

(a) A standard security is a charge over land. It must be registered in the Register of Sasines or the Land Register as the case may be. It is granted by Eve in favour of the lender and serves to prevent Eve selling the cottage without first obtaining the discharge of the standard security, unless the purchaser is unwise enough to buy the cottage subject to Eve's standard security, which would be unlikely. The standard security will normally only be discharged once the lender has been repaid its loan, interest and any expenses. If Eve fails to maintain what would in England be called her mortgage payments, the lender could take the steps open to it in terms of the standard security documentation to repossess the cottage, evict Eve and her belongings and sell the cottage. Alternatively, the lender could foreclose on the property, which is to sell the property with the intention of keeping it for itself, thus preventing Eve from redeeming the property. If there is a tenant in the cottage (of which the lender was aware), the lender could receive the rents from the tenant as part of its right under the standard security. If there is an unauthorised tenant, the tenant could be evicted by the lender prior to the repossession of the property.

(b) In this situation, the bank could either receive a pledge of the wine in the vats in the warehouse, or it could be given a floating charge. If there is a pledge, the vats must be clearly identifiable, separated from other persons' vats, and physically unavailable to Eve's company (perhaps by being fenced off and locked, with the key being given to the bank) except with the express permission of the bank as its agent for such necessary purposes as, say, maintenance. It must not be open to Eve's company to abstract wine from time to time and to bottle and sell it (see *West Lothian Oil Co. (in liquidation) v. Mair*). This would give the bank a fixed charge over the wine and would be good against a liquidator or any creditor.

A more common remedy would be for the company to grant a floating charge over the company's assets, including the wine in the vats. By this means the company would have much greater freedom to continue dealing in the wine. Providing the company's net assets were always greater than the value of the loan, the bank would be unlikely to have any difficulty with this. If the company defaulted on the repayment of the loan, the bank would appoint a receiver under the Insolvency Act 1986, s. 52, who would proceed to sell the wine, and any other asset of the company caught by the crystallised floating charge, to recoup the loss to the bank, subject to payment of any prior-ranking claims, including preferential debts, under the Insolvency Act 1986, s. 60.

A floating charge would need to be registered at the office of the Registrar of Companies within 21 days of its creation (Companies Act 1985, s. 410). Without registration the floating charge would be void against another creditor, liquidator or administrator. The pledge of the wine is an unregistrable charge and would only be registered in the company's own register of charges, not in the public register available at the office of the Registrar of Companies.

6. *Jim, a tradesman, is unfortunately in financial difficulties. He has total assets of £60,000, of which the major part is his own home which he shares with his wife. The house is entirely in his own name and is worth £40,000. He owns no other heritage, though he leases a lock-up garage which is owned by a small company, Keepo Ltd, and he pays them rent of £300 a month. In the garage he keeps the tools of this trade and some antique furniture that he is hoping to restore. Sadly he has been getting no business recently and he has not been paying his bills.*

*By June 1, 1999 the following matters have arisen:*

*(a) he is three months behind on the rent for the garage;*
*(b) he has transferred his home to his wife by means of a disposition recorded in the Register of Sasines on May 1, 1999;*
*(c) on May 20, 1999 he has repaid to his brother, Tom, a loan of £5,000 which according to the terms of their loan agreement was not due to be repaid until March 1, 2000;*
*(d) he is due to pay Tools-R-Us Ltd £3,000 for various items, the payment date being April 1, 1999;*
*(e) he has failed to account to H.M. Customs and Excise for the sum of £4,000 in respect of outstanding VAT also due on April 1, 1999;*
*(f) Big Supplies plc, which had not received payment of the sum of £5,000, have arrested his bank account with the Bank of Inchcolm and have obtained funds from it by an action of furthcoming on May 15, 1999;*
*(g) Join Us, a loan shark, has insisted that the £5,000 loan Jim borrowed from him at a rate of 10 per cent per annum should now have its interest rate increased to 20 per cent to take account of Jim's uncertain financial prospects.*

*Jim's accountant successfully petitions the court for an award of sequestration dated June 1, 1999, against Jim on the grounds that he failed to pay outstanding accounting fees of £3,000.*

*Under these circumstances, what points of law apply to (a) to (g)?*

This question refers to bankruptcy which is governed by the Bankruptcy (Scotland) Act 1985 ("BSA"). Jim is sequestrated with effect from June 1, 1999 and an interim trustee will be appointed to safeguard his assets; in due course a permanent trustee will be vested in those assets. Given the size of the assets it is possible that he could repay in full all his creditors, but from the information given it would appear that he is both practically insolvent and by virtue of the award of sequestration apparently insolvent.

(a) If Keepo Ltd proceeds to a sequestration for rent, the landlord's hypothec will defeat the trustee in sequestration (BSA, s. 33(2)). Accordingly the landlord would ultimately be able to seize and sell the antique furniture in the garage, though not the tools of Jim's trade.

(b) As the disposition in favour of his wife took place one month before the date of sequestration, it falls within the five-year period required for a gratuitous alienation to an associate (BSA, s. 34). The trustee could apply to court to reduce the disposition and have the house returned to the debtor's estate. The trustee could not necessarily immediately force Jim and his wife out of the house since they need somewhere to live, but ultimately, if necessary, the trustee may be able to force the sale of the house (BSA, s. 40), subject to the court's protection of Jim's family.

(c) This repayment would be an unfair preference under the BSA, s. 36 and Tom would be required to return the loan. Tom would merely become an ordinary creditor.

(d) Tools-R-Us are merely ordinary creditors. They obtain no privileged position relative to other creditors.

(e) By contrast, H.M. Customs and Excise are preferred creditors and will be repaid out of the debtor's estate in priority to the ordinary creditors (BSA, s. 51(1)(e)).

(f) Sequestration acts as if a completed diligence for all creditors had taken place simultaneously on the date of sequestration. Big Supplies plc are effectively ordinary creditors, but they will be able to obtain their expenses (BSA, s. 37(5)). The diligence they effected will be equalised with all the other creditors.

(g) This is an extortionate credit transaction and the court could insist that the terms of the loan be rewritten and that the creditor only be entitled to a reasonable rate of interest (BSA, s. 61).

*7. Consider the points of law arising out of the following situation:*

*Martin's electronics business has just completed 10 successful years, and he wishes to have a large and splendid garden party to celebrate. While he is confident in the realm of computers, he is less so in the realm of corporate hospitality, and so asks Senga to organise the party for him, as he does not have time to arrange all the details himself. He explains that he wants marquees, plenty of good quality wine, canapés, children's entertainments, loudspeakers, etc.*

*As Martin has a high opinion of Senga he asks her personally to arrange all this for him. He gives her a budget and expects her to keep within it. There is no mention of a fee for her services in the budget, and when she asks about her fee, he says he will get back to her about that but fails to do so.*

*Senga's little brother, Sam, is just trying to set up his lighting business and she asks him to set up the lighting and sound system. She asks him for a commission of only 5 per cent (she would normally have asked 10 per cent) for offering him the work. Her other brother, Bill, runs a marquee erection and hire service through a limited company, in which she has a 25 per cent shareholding, and she asks him to put up the marquees. Although Martin did not ask her to do so, she arranged for floodlighting of the grounds and for a water feature to serve as a backdrop to the evening.*

*Come the evening, the party goes very well until the unfortunate moment when Martin drops a glass of water and fatally electrocutes himself. As none of his family is with him, everyone looks to Senga to sort things out. As the band will not leave until they have been paid, she pays them out of her own pocket since they inevitably want cash.*

*After the funeral the bills for the party come in. Martin's executors have misgivings about some of the items and announce that until Senga produces proper accounts no funds will be disbursed to her or anyone else.*

This question is about agency. There are no special requirements for creating a contract of agency, and although there is no sum set down for her remuneration Senga would normally be entitled to be paid on a *quantum meruit* basis in the absence of any agreement to the contrary.

However, she has not necessarily exercised her fiduciary duty to Martin in the way that she should. She obtained a secret profit from her brother (as in *Boston Deep Sea Fishing Ltd v. Ansell* (1888)) which should properly have been disclosed to Martin. Likewise her interest in the marquee company run by Bill should have been disclosed to Martin for his approval, since there is a conflict of interest there as well (see *McPherson's Trs v. Watt* (1877)). Her use of the floodlighting and water feature raises the issue of whether she had the apparent authority to hire such items on Martin's behalf. The question does not state whether he approved of these items, but if he did, he would be deemed to have ratified her actions, in which case Martin's estate would be liable for their cost. Even if he did not approve, and if the floodlight and water feature installers had no reason to think that these items were not within Senga's authority to order, and the estate would still be liable (see *Watteau v. Fenwick* (1892)). When Senga paid the band's fees following Martin's sudden death it is arguable that she was acting as an agent of necessity as something had to be done in a hurry and there was no one with the requisite authority to act on his or his estate's behalf.

Finally it is certainly the case that Senga would need to produce accounts for all her intromissions and expenditure, this being part of her general duty to Martin and the estate.

8. *Three sisters, Effie, Ishbel and Morag wish to set up a laundry business. The idea is that they will visit clients' houses, uplift the clients' laundry and deliver it to them the same day cleaned, ironed, and sorted out. They open a partnership account and each put in £200. They buy a new washing machine, tumble drier, iron and ironing board. All the work is done in Effie's house, as she has the biggest laundry room; the collection and delivery is done in Ishbel's car; while Morag, who is the most personable, is the one who deals with the clients on the telephone and in person. They call their business "The Three Graces".*

*Although after six months the business is showing a certain profit, it is not enough for Effie's liking. She takes it upon herself to branch out into other forms of cleaning, such as dry-cleaning furniture and repairing clothes. She does not tell her sisters about this, even though most of her customers came through the business. She also asks her husband, Donald, to help her, and when he does so he is inclined to refer to "our business, The Three Graces". Sometimes he even signs receipts on behalf of the firm for the work that Effie is doing. One day he does this, but it turns out that Effie has made a sad mess of the work she has done. The owner of the badly repaired furniture is proposing to sue the firm. Ishbel and Morag are furious when they hear of this and say that Donald had no business signing receipts on behalf of the firm and that he alone is liable. Unfortunately Donald is bankrupt, as the client is well aware.*

*Ishbel believes that as she is doing all the driving and she is paying for the petrol she should be entitled to a greater share of the profits than the one-third share which they have verbally agreed they each should take out from the business. She also believes that the wear and tear on the car and her insurance is not being properly recompensed, so she takes money out of the bank account whenever she is a bit short. She is not very good about keeping records of her withdrawals from the bank account. When challenged she claims that she is repaying herself her expenses, not receiving her drawings.*

*Morag decides that in her free time she should set up an escort agency, and believing that a bank would be unlikely to fund her, she approaches a small local finance shop for funds. She explains what she needs the money for, and the finance shop says that it will lend her the money provided the finance shop can have a deposit from the firm of The Three Graces and that the firm will pay an interest rate of 17 per cent. Morag explains that she cannot produce a deposit, but she on behalf of the firm will give the finance shop a promissory note undertaking to repay the capital sum and interest at the desired rate. Morag fails to tell her sisters about the promissory note, but shortly before the due date for repayment of the promissory note Effie disappears with all the firm's funds anyway.*

*What is the legal position relating to all this ?*

When Effie embarks on another business she will probably try to say that it is unconnected with the business of The Three Graces. On the other hand, under the Partnership Act 1890, s. 29, she should disclose any private profits accruing to her through the use of the partnership's business connection and name. She would be required to hand over any secret profits to the firm. It is arguable that the failure to prevent Donald representing himself as authorised to sign documents, even though it was not with the approval of Ishbel and Morag, could be construed as holding Donald out to be authorised. As far as the annoyed client is concerned she had no reason to doubt that Donald was authorised, and would be able to assert her rights under the Partnership Act, s. 14 since she believed that Donald was either a partner, or, under general rules of agency, that he had apparent authority to do as he was doing. As Donald is not worth suing, it makes sense for the client to sue the partnership since it could probably satisfy her decree. If the partnership assets were insufficient, each partner would be jointly and severally liable to the client for the debt arising from the client's claim (Partnership Act 1890, s. 9).

As regards Ishbel, she has forgotten that there is a duty on each partner under the Partnership Act 1890, s. 28 to render true accounts and disclose all things affecting the partnership. She should be keeping proper records, and although she is indeed entitled to her expenses under section 24(2) (in the absence of any rules to the contrary), this does not give her permission to treat the accounts lightly.

Morag's loan cannot be described as being in the ordinary course of business, and accordingly under the Partnership Act, s. 5 there is no reason for the partnership to be liable as it must have been apparent, on the principle of *Paterson Bros v. Gladstone* (1891) that Morag was not authorised to pledge the firm's credit in this way. So the firm would not be liable anyway, which is probably just as well since Effie has taken all its money. The two other sisters could sue Effie for the money if they can find her.

9. *Emmeline, Fingal and Genista run a partnership together making tartan souvenirs for tourists. On their accountants' advice they decide to incorporate the business as a limited liability company. All had been equal partners, but for various domestic reasons, Emmeline decides that she wants to subscribe for only a few shares in the company, though she is willing to lend money to the company.*

*The company has an authorised share capital of £1,000. Emmeline takes 100 shares of £1.00 each and Fingal and Genista take 450 shares of £1.00. Emmeline agrees to lend £3,500 to the company in the form of a loan repayable in five years' time with a coupon of 8 per cent. All three shareholders are appointed directors.*

*The company starts to trade with Table A as its articles of association. Negotiations continue between the shareholders. It is thought appropriate that Emmeline should obtain some security for her loan. It is also agreed that all decisions taken by the directors should be unanimous and that no other shareholders should be admitted without the consent of all shareholders. However, no documentation is ever finalised or signed to reflect these agreements as none of the three has time to look at these matters in detail.*

*Almost immediately after incorporation problems arise. Emmeline wishes to withdraw her money from the company.*

*What should have been done, but was not, and what could be done now? Advise the three directors.*

## What should have been done

In an ideal world, the company should have drawn up its own version of its articles, based on Table A, but altered to reflect the desires of the three shareholders. Given that Emmeline has fewer shares than the others, it would have been sensible for her to have a class of shares whose rights could not have been altered by the other two shareholders (Companies Act 1985, s. 125). One of the rights attaching to her shares would have been that the other shareholders may not improve their own rights (since the other shareholders effectively are a class of shares in their own right too) relative to hers. Any alteration of their rights would require her approval. The second thing to build in would be weighted voting (on the principle of *Bushell v. Faith* (1970)), so that no two shareholders could "gang up" on the third. This would effectively also force the shareholders to work in concert. An alternative method would be to have three classes of shares with a deadlock agreement forcing them to vote unanimously or not at all, failing which the issue could be referred to arbitration or the company could be wound up.

If Emmeline wishes to have security for her loan, she may do this, and she could have a standard security over heritage, if the company has any, or a floating charge over its assets. The problem with a floating charge is that if it is granted within two years of the company's insolvent liquidation, the floating charge may be reducible at the instance of the liquidator because Emmeline is a "connected person" ; hence the loan must be genuinely made for value to the company (Insolvency Act 1986, s. 245). Notwithstanding this caveat, there is no reason why she should not have the benefit of a charge, but if it is to be a standard security in her favour, it must be registered within 21 days of the registration of the standard security in the Register of Sasines or Land Register (as the case may be) or, if a floating charge, 21 days from the date of execution of the floating charge (Companies Act 1985, s. 410). Assuming the charge is validly registered, then in the event of the company's insolvency she could sell the heritable property or appoint a receiver (Insolvency Act 1986, s. 51).

**The current position**
Under the existing circumstances, the best thing to do would be to wind up the company following a voluntary resolution to that effect under the Insolvency Act 1986, s. 84(1)(b). If the company is solvent, all the creditors will be repaid and everyone should get their money back. It is open to Emmeline to petition the court for a winding-up order for repayment of her loan (Insolvency Act 1986, s. 122(1)(f)), but it would clearly be an expensive way for the company of getting her money back, not least because there would be court fees on top of a liquidator's fees to deal with.

# INDEX